Almeria Travel Guide 2025

Almere Uncovered: A Travel Guide to the City's Top Attractions and Hidden Gems

JAXON JOY

Copyright 2025 Jaxon Joy.

All right reserved. No part of this publication may be reproduced,stored in a retrieval system,or transmitted in any form or by any means,electronic,mechanical,photocopying,recording,or otherwise,without prior written permission of the copyright owner.

TABLE OF CONTENTS

Chapter 1: Introduction to Almería — 7
   1.1 Overview of Almería — 8
   1.2 Historical Background and Cultural Influence — 9
   1.3 Geographic and Climate Features — 11
   1.4 How to Get to Almería — 12
   1.5 Best Time to Visit — 13

Chapter 2: The Rich History of Almería — 13
   2.1 The Islamic Era and the Alcazaba Fortress — 14
      The Alcazaba: Almería's Crown Jewel — 15
   2.2 Christian Reconquest and Catholic Influence — 16
   2.3 Almería's Role in the Spanish Civil War — 18
   2.4 Architectural Heritage and Preserved Sites — 19

Chapter 3: Top Attractions in Almería — 20
   3.1 The Alcazaba of Almería: A Moorish Masterpiece — 21
   3.2 The Cathedral of Almería: A Fortress of Faith — 23
      What to See Inside the Cathedral — 25
   3.3 The English Cable: An Industrial Wonder — 25
   3.4 Almería's Historic Old Town: A Walk Through Time — 26

Chapter 4: Exploring Almería's Coastline — 27
   4.1 Best Beaches: Playa de los Genoveses, Playa de Mónsul, and More — 29
   4.2 Water Sports and Activities: Diving, Kayaking, and Sailing — 31
   4.3 Coastal Villages and Hidden Coves — 33
      Níjar: A Traditional Andalusian Gem — 33
      Las Negras: A Bohemian Beach Town — 33

Aguamarga: A Hidden Coastal Retreat   33

Chapter 5: Natural Wonders and Outdoor Adventures   35

5.1 Cabo de Gata-Níjar Natural Park   36

5.2 Sierra Alhamilla and Desert Landscapes   37

The Tabernas Desert: Spain's Only True Desert   38

5.3 Hiking and Eco-Tourism Activities   39

Top Hiking Trails in Almería   39

Sustainable Tourism and Eco-Friendly Adventures   39

5.4 Birdwatching and Wildlife Exploration   40

Chapter 6: Almería's Unique Film Heritage   42

6.1 How Almería Became the Hollywood of Europe   43

6.2 Famous Movies Filmed in Almería   44

6.3 The Western Theme Parks: Oasys Mini Hollywood, Fort Bravo, and Texas Hollywood   46

6.4 Film Tourism and Thematic Tours   47

Chapter 7: Gastronomy and Local Cuisine   49

7.1 Traditional Almerían Dishes   50

7.2 The Best Tapas Bars in Almería   51

7.3 Seafood and Coastal Culinary Delights   53

7.4 Food Markets and Authentic Dining Experiences   54

Chapter 8: Wine and Local Beverages   56

8.1 The Wine Regions of Almería   57

8.2 Bodegas and Wine Tasting Experiences   59

8.3 Traditional Drinks of the Region   60

8.4 Olive Oil and Other Local Specialties   61

Chapter 9: Cultural Events and Festivals 64
   9.1 Semana Santa and Religious Celebrations 65
   9.2 Feria de Almería: The Grand Annual Festival 66
   9.3 Music and Art Festivals 68
   9.4 Local Traditions and Folklore 69

Chapter 10: Shopping and Handicrafts in Almería 71
   10.1 Best Shopping Streets and Local Markets 72
   10.2 Traditional Crafts: Ceramics, Pottery, and Textiles 74
      Ceramics and Pottery: A Legacy of the Moors 74
   10.3 Where to Buy Authentic Souvenirs 76
   10.4 Modern Shopping Malls and Boutiques 77

Chapter 11: Day Trips and Excursions 79
   11.1 Mojácar: The Whitewashed Village on the Hills 80
   11.2 Roquetas de Mar: A Coastal Getaway 81
   11.3 Tabernas Desert and its Western Film Sets 82
   11.4 Exploring Alpujarra Almeriense 84

Chapter 12: Nightlife and Entertainment 86
   12.1 Best Bars and Nightclubs in Almería 87
   12.2 Flamenco Shows and Live Music Venues 88
      Where to Experience Authentic Flamenco in Almería 88
      Best Live Music Bars in Almería 89
   12.3 Open-Air Cinemas and Cultural Performances 89
   12.4 Late-Night Tapas Culture 91

Chapter 13: Family-Friendly Almería 93
   13.1 Top Attractions for Kids 94

13.2 Family Beaches and Outdoor Parks　　96
13.3 Interactive Museums and Educational Activities
　　97
13.4 Best Family-Friendly Accommodations　　98
Chapter 14: Sustainable and Responsible Tourism in Almería　　100
14.1 Eco-Friendly Travel Tips　　101
14.2 Supporting Local Businesses and Artisans　102
14.3 Conservation Efforts in Almería　　104
14.4 Ethical Wildlife and Nature Experiences　106
Chapter 15: Practical Travel Information　　107
15.1 Transportation Options Within Almería　108
15.2 Safety Tips and Emergency Contacts　　110
15.3 Local Customs and Etiquette　　112
15.4 Budgeting and Cost-Saving Travel Tips　113
Chapter 16: Conclusion and Final Thoughts　115
16.1 Capturing the Spirit of Almería　　116
16.2 Resources for Further Reading　　118
16.3 Inspirational Quotes About Almería　　120
16.4 Reflecting on Your Journey　　121
Final Thoughts　　122

Chapter 1: Introduction to Almería

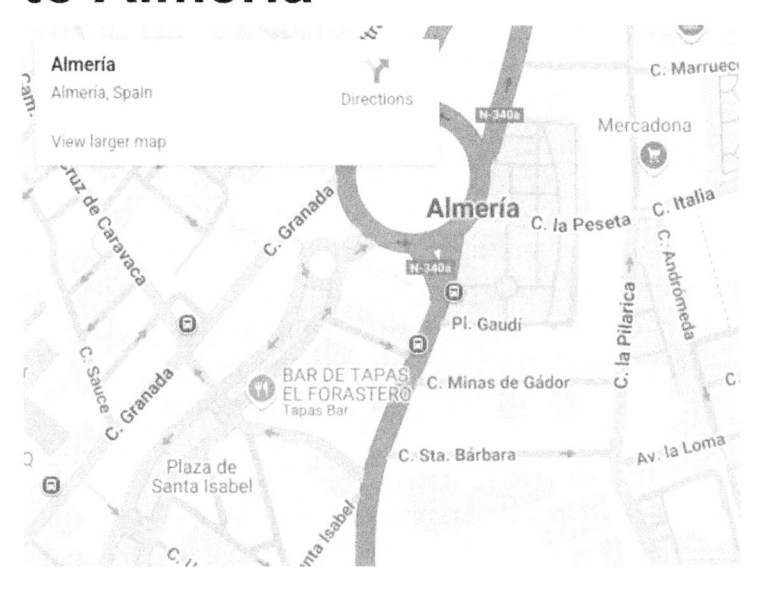

Almería is one of Spain's most enchanting yet often overlooked destinations. Nestled in the southeastern corner of the country, it boasts a unique blend of **stunning coastline, rich history, and a distinctive desert landscape** unlike anywhere else in Spain. From its impressive **Moorish fortress** to its sun-kissed Mediterranean beaches, Almería captivates travelers with its **authentic charm and diverse attractions**. Whether you are a history buff, a nature lover, or a foodie in search of the region's best tapas, this city has something to offer for everyone.

In this chapter, we will take a closer look at Almería's identity, from its **historical roots and cultural influences** to its **geographical wonders and climate**. We will also explore **the best ways to reach the city** and determine **the perfect time to visit**, depending on your travel preferences.

1.1 Overview of Almería

Almería is the **capital of the province of the same name** in Andalusia, Spain's southernmost autonomous community. Known for its **year-round sunshine**, the city is one of Spain's warmest regions, making it an ideal destination for travelers seeking warm weather and outdoor adventures.

The name "Almería" derives from the Arabic **"Al-Mariyya,"** meaning **"The Watchtower"**, a reference to its historical role as a strategic coastal defense point during the Moorish rule. Today, Almería is a blend of its **ancient past and modern charm**, where medieval fortresses stand alongside contemporary city life.

Some of the city's highlights include:

- The **Alcazaba of Almería**, one of the largest Moorish fortresses in Spain
- The **Cabo de Gata-Níjar Natural Park**, a haven for nature lovers
- A coastline boasting **some of Spain's most untouched and picturesque beaches**

- A **strong cinematic heritage**, with Hollywood blockbusters like *Indiana Jones and the Last Crusade* and *Lawrence of Arabia* filmed in its desert landscapes

Despite its beauty, Almería remains **one of Spain's lesser-known tourist destinations**, making it perfect for travelers who wish to **avoid large crowds** and experience an **authentic Andalusian atmosphere**.

Modern Era and Film Industry Boom

1.2 Historical Background and Cultural Influence

Almería's history is a **tapestry woven with diverse civilizations**, each leaving a lasting impact on the city's architecture, traditions, and identity.

Prehistoric and Roman Influence

Long before the Moors arrived, the region around Almería was home to **Iberian tribes** and later became part of the **Roman Empire**. The city's strategic location along the Mediterranean made it an important trading hub. Ruins from this era can still be found in and around Almería, hinting at its Roman past.

Moorish Almería and the Golden Age

Almería **flourished under Moorish rule** from the 10th to the 15th centuries. In **955 AD**, Abd al-Rahman III, the **Caliph of Córdoba**, fortified the city and built the **Alcazaba**, which became a powerful military stronghold. During this time, Almería thrived as a center of **commerce, art, and science**, exporting luxurious goods like **silk, ceramics, and gold**.

Christian Reconquest and Catholic Influence

In **1489**, the Catholic Monarchs, **Queen Isabella I of Castile and King Ferdinand II of Aragon**, conquered Almería as part of the **Reconquista**. The city saw an influx of **Christian influence**, with **mosques converted into churches** and **new Catholic structures** built, including the **Almería Cathedral**, which was designed to withstand pirate attacks.

In the **20th century**, Almería gained international fame as a **filming location** for Hollywood movies. The **Tabernas Desert**, located nearby, became the perfect setting for **Spaghetti Westerns**, attracting directors like **Sergio Leone**. Films such as *The Good, The Bad, and The Ugly* were shot here, cementing Almería's legacy in the film industry.

Today, Almería **preserves its rich cultural heritage** while embracing modernity. Its unique blend of **Moorish, Christian, and Mediterranean influences** makes it one of Spain's most fascinating destinations.

1.3 Geographic and Climate Features

Almería is distinguished by **three primary geographical features**: its **coastline, mountains, and desert landscapes**.

Coastline and Beaches

Almería is home to some of **Spain's most unspoiled beaches**, particularly in the **Cabo de Gata-Níjar Natural Park**. With **crystal-clear waters, golden sands, and hidden coves**, this coastline is a paradise for **swimmers, divers, and nature lovers**.

Mountains and Natural Parks

To the north, the **Sierra Alhamilla Mountains** rise above the city, offering breathtaking views and opportunities for **hiking and nature excursions**.

Tabernas Desert: The Only Desert in Europe

Just a short drive from the city, the **Tabernas Desert** is a landscape **straight out of a Wild West movie**. Known as **Europe's only desert**, it is characterized by **arid plains, dramatic rock formations, and sparse vegetation**.

Climate: The Sunniest City in Europe

Almería enjoys a **Mediterranean desert climate**, with **hot summers, mild winters, and minimal rainfall**. The city receives **over 3,000 hours of sunshine per year**, making it **one of the sunniest places in Europe**.

1.4 How to Get to Almería

By Air

- **Almería Airport (LEI)** offers **direct flights** from major Spanish cities like Madrid and Barcelona, as well as some European destinations.

By Train

- The **AVE high-speed train** is not yet available to Almería, but **regular trains** connect the city to **Madrid, Seville, and Granada**.

By Bus

- Affordable **long-distance buses** run from cities like **Malaga, Granada, and Madrid**.

By Car

- If you prefer a scenic drive, the **A-7 coastal highway** offers **breathtaking sea views** while connecting Almería to other Andalusian cities.

1.5 Best Time to Visit

The best time to visit depends on **your travel goals**:

- **Spring (March to May)** – Perfect for **exploring historic sites** and enjoying **mild weather**.
- **Summer (June to August)** – Ideal for **beach lovers** but expect **high temperatures**.
- **Autumn (September to November)** – A **sweet spot** for **fewer crowds and warm sea temperatures**.
- **Winter (December to February)** – A **quiet season** with **mild weather**, perfect for **hiking and sightseeing**.

For those who want to **experience local culture**, visiting during the **Feria de Almería in August** or **Semana Santa in Spring** is highly recommended.

Chapter 2: The Rich History of Almería

Almería is a city shaped by centuries of conquest, cultural exchange, and resilience. Its history is a fascinating blend of **Moorish grandeur, Christian influence, and war-time struggles**, leaving behind an architectural and cultural legacy that continues to define the city today. From the towering **Alcazaba fortress**, a symbol of its Islamic past, to the scars left by the **Spanish Civil War**, Almería's history is deeply embedded in its streets, buildings, and traditions.

In this chapter, we will delve into Almería's **Islamic Golden Age**, the **Christian Reconquest**, its role during the **Spanish Civil War**, and its **rich architectural heritage** that still stands today.

2.1 The Islamic Era and the Alcazaba Fortress

The history of Almería took a dramatic turn in the 10th century when it became a **flourishing Islamic stronghold** under **Moorish rule**. During this period, the city transformed into a **bustling port, a center of trade, and a hub for art and science**.

The Rise of Almería Under the Moors

In **955 AD**, **Abd al-Rahman III**, the Caliph of Córdoba, **fortified the city and built the Alcazaba**, making Almería one of the most important defensive settlements along the Mediterranean coast. The city became a **key**

maritime center, exporting luxury goods such as **silk, ceramics, and textiles** across the Islamic world.

Almería thrived as part of **Al-Andalus**, the Muslim-ruled territory in Spain, enjoying **economic prosperity, architectural advancements, and cultural exchanges** with North Africa and the Middle East.

The Alcazaba: Almería's Crown Jewel

One of the most iconic remnants of Almería's Islamic past is the **Alcazaba, a massive fortress overlooking the city**.

- The Alcazaba is **the second-largest Moorish fortress in Spain**, after the **Alhambra in Granada**.
- It was designed to **protect the city from naval and land-based invasions**, offering **panoramic views of the coast and surrounding mountains**.
- The fortress was **self-sufficient**, containing **palaces, gardens, baths, and even a mosque**.
- Its **three enclosures** included military barracks, royal residences, and defense structures.

Even today, walking through the **Alcazaba's ancient walls** feels like stepping back in time. The fortress **showcases intricate Islamic architecture**, including **horseshoe arches, geometric patterns, and courtyards reminiscent of Moorish palaces**.

The Fall of Islamic Almería

Despite its strength, Almería's Golden Age did not last forever. In the **11th century**, internal conflicts weakened **Muslim-ruled Spain**, and Almería fell under different rulers, including the **Almoravids and Almohads**. Eventually, in **1489**, the Catholic Monarchs **Ferdinand and Isabella** conquered the city, marking the end of **Islamic rule in Almería**.

2.2 Christian Reconquest and Catholic Influence

The Catholic Monarchs and the Conversion of Almería

When **Queen Isabella I of Castile and King Ferdinand II of Aragon** seized Almería in **1489**, they ushered in a **new era of Catholic rule**. The **Reconquista**, or Christian reconquest of Spain, saw the conversion of **mosques into churches**, the destruction of many **Islamic cultural landmarks**, and the introduction of **Catholic traditions**.

The Transformation of Almería Cathedral

One of the most striking examples of this transformation is the **Cathedral of Almería**.

- Originally built as a **mosque**, it was converted into a **Catholic church** following the Reconquest.
- Unlike most traditional cathedrals, the **Almería Cathedral** was designed as a **fortress**, with **thick walls, towers, and defensive elements** to protect it from **Berber pirate attacks** from North Africa.
- Inside, the cathedral **blends Gothic, Renaissance, and Baroque styles**, reflecting the **religious and artistic changes brought by Christian rule**.

Religious Shifts and Inquisition

With Catholicism firmly established, **Muslims and Jews** faced **forced conversions, persecution, and expulsion** under the Spanish **Inquisition**. Many residents who **converted to Christianity** (known as **Moriscos**) continued to practice **Islamic traditions in secret** but were eventually expelled in the early **17th century**.

The Catholic rule left a profound mark on Almería's **architecture, traditions, and identity**, making it a **deeply religious city** with grand **churches, monasteries, and Christian festivals** that continue today.

2.3 Almería's Role in the Spanish Civil War

Fast forward to the **20th century**, and Almería once again found itself at the heart of Spanish conflict. The **Spanish Civil War (1936-1939)** was one of the most devastating periods in **Spain's modern history**, and Almería, though relatively small, was deeply affected.

Almería as a Republican Stronghold

During the war, Almería was a **Republican city**, meaning it supported **Spain's democratic government against Francisco Franco's Nationalist forces**.

- The city was **one of the last Republican strongholds**, holding out against Franco's army longer than many other Spanish cities.
- It was **heavily bombed** by **German and Italian forces** allied with Franco, suffering **significant destruction**.

The Bombardment of Almería by Nazi Germany

One of the darkest chapters in Almería's history was the **Nazi attack on the city in 1937**.

- On **May 31, 1937**, Nazi **warships bombarded Almería**, causing widespread devastation.
- This was **one of the first examples of modern naval warfare** targeting a civilian population.

- The attack left **hundreds dead and destroyed much of the city's historical architecture.**

Legacy of the War

Today, **Almería still bears the scars of the Civil War.** Many of its **underground air raid shelters**, used to protect civilians from bombings, have been **preserved as museums,** allowing visitors to **experience the reality of life during the war.**

2.4 Architectural Heritage and Preserved Sites

Despite its turbulent past, Almería **boasts an impressive collection of historical sites** that reflect its **multi-layered history**. Some of the city's most remarkable **architectural landmarks** include:

The Alcazaba of Almería

- A **testament to Islamic engineering** and one of the city's top attractions.
- Offers **panoramic views** of Almería's old town and coastline.

Almería Cathedral

- A **one-of-a-kind cathedral-fortress**, built to **defend against pirate attacks.**

- Features a **mix of Gothic, Renaissance, and Baroque designs**.

Civil War Shelters of Almería

- A network of **underground tunnels** that **protected civilians during air raids**.
- Now open to the public as a **historical museum**.

The English Cable (Cable Inglés)

- A **historic iron pier**, built in the early **20th century** by **British engineers** for **exporting minerals**.
- One of Almería's most **unusual and striking industrial landmarks**.

Tabernas Desert and Film Studios

- Home to **Europe's only desert**.
- Famous for its **Hollywood Western film sets**, including those used in *The Good, The Bad, and The Ugly*.

Chapter 3: Top Attractions in Almería

Almería is a city that blends **Moorish history, Christian heritage, and modern influences**, offering a fascinating mix of **ancient fortresses, grand cathedrals, and industrial marvels**. Walking through its streets is like stepping into a **living history book**, where every corner tells a story of conquest, trade, and resilience.

In this chapter, we will explore **four of Almería's must-see landmarks**:

- **The Alcazaba**, a breathtaking Moorish fortress that stands as a symbol of Almería's past.
- **The Cathedral of Almería**, a unique structure that combines religious grandeur with defensive architecture.
- **The English Cable**, a fascinating reminder of the city's industrial era.
- **Almería's Old Town**, where history comes alive in its narrow streets, charming squares, and hidden courtyards.

Whether you're a **history enthusiast, an architecture lover, or simply a traveler looking to immerse yourself in Spanish culture**, these attractions will leave you **enchanted by Almería's unique charm**.

3.1 The Alcazaba of Almería: A Moorish Masterpiece

Towering over the city, the **Alcazaba of Almería** is the **largest Muslim fortress in Spain**, second only to the

Alhambra in Granada. Built in **955 AD** by **Caliph Abd al-Rahman III**, this massive stronghold was designed to **protect the city from invaders** and serve as a **political and military hub**.

A Journey Through the Alcazaba's Three Enclosures

The **Alcazaba** is divided into **three sections**, each built during different historical periods:

1. **The First Enclosure** – This section housed **troops, military barracks, and water reservoirs**. It was designed for **defense and survival**, ensuring that the fortress could withstand long sieges. Today, visitors can explore the remains of **guard towers and ancient walls**, offering a glimpse into the fortress's military past.

2. **The Second Enclosure** – This area was **home to Moorish rulers** and their courts. It once featured **lavish palaces, lush gardens, and intricate Islamic architecture**. Though time has worn down much of its splendor, **restored sections of courtyards and archways** still reflect the beauty of **Andalusian craftsmanship**.

3. **The Third Enclosure** – This part of the fortress was added **after the Christian conquest of**

Almería in 1489. The **Catholic Monarchs built a new fortress with European-style battlements**, integrating **Renaissance and Gothic influences** into the Alcazaba's Islamic foundation.

Why Visit the Alcazaba?

- **Breathtaking Views:** From its towers, you get **panoramic vistas of Almería, the Mediterranean Sea, and the rugged mountains beyond**.
- **Architectural Marvels:** The fortress **blends Moorish, Gothic, and Renaissance elements**, showcasing the **evolution of Spanish architecture**.
- **Historical Significance:** The Alcazaba tells the story of **Almería's past rulers**, from the **Moors to the Catholic Monarchs**.

Exploring the Alcazaba is like stepping into a **real-life medieval epic**, where **history, legend, and breathtaking scenery** come together in one unforgettable experience.

3.2 The Cathedral of Almería: A Fortress of Faith

Unlike most traditional Spanish cathedrals, the **Cathedral of Almería** is as much a **fortress** as it is a place of worship. Built in **1524**, this unique structure was designed to **defend the city against pirate raids**, which were a constant threat along the Mediterranean coast.

A Cathedral Like No Other

The **Almería Cathedral** is one of Spain's most **unusual religious buildings**, and here's why:

- **Defensive Architecture:** Instead of the typical **elegant spires and delicate carvings**, the cathedral features **thick stone walls, watchtowers, and battlements**, resembling a **military fortress**.
- **Blend of Styles:** Inside, the cathedral combines **Gothic, Renaissance, and Baroque elements**, creating an **awe-inspiring interior** with intricate altars and stained-glass windows.
- **Legends and Mysteries:** The cathedral is home to **an ancient organ, religious relics, and hidden passageways** once used to escape pirate attacks.

The Pirate Invasions and the Cathedral's Role

During the **16th century**, Almería was frequently attacked by **Berber pirates from North Africa**. To **protect both the clergy and the city's residents**, the cathedral was built with **high walls, defensive towers, and even a fortified entrance**. This allowed it to function as a **safe haven during enemy raids**.

What to See Inside the Cathedral

- **The High Altar:** A stunning example of **Spanish Baroque artistry**, featuring intricate carvings and religious iconography.
- **The Cloisters:** Peaceful courtyards that offer a glimpse into **monastic life in medieval Spain**.
- **The Side Chapels:** Each chapel tells a different story, with **paintings, sculptures, and religious relics** dating back centuries.

Visiting the **Cathedral of Almería** is a journey through **faith, history, and military strategy**, all wrapped into one magnificent building.

3.3 The English Cable: An Industrial Wonder

At first glance, the **English Cable (Cable Inglés)** might seem out of place in a city known for its **Moorish and Catholic heritage**. But this impressive **iron pier**, built in **1904**, is a **testament to Almería's industrial past**.

A Legacy of British Engineering

The **English Cable** was constructed by the **British mining company "The Alquife Iron Ore Company"** to transport **iron ore from the mines of Almería to ships in the Mediterranean**.

- The pier is a **remarkable example of 20th-century industrial architecture**, influenced by the designs of **Gustave Eiffel**.
- It played a crucial role in **Almería's mining boom**, helping to **export tons of minerals** to the rest of Europe.

Why It's Worth a Visit

- **A Fascinating Slice of History:** The pier symbolizes Almería's **economic and industrial transformation**.
- **Unique Photography Spot:** Its **rustic iron structure** against the blue Mediterranean makes for **stunning pictures**.
- **Sunset Walks:** The area around the **English Cable** is perfect for a **leisurely stroll along the waterfront**, offering a mix of **history and scenic beauty**.

3.4 Almería's Historic Old Town: A Walk Through Time

No visit to Almería is complete without wandering through its **historic Old Town**, a labyrinth of **narrow** streets, whitewashed buildings, and hidden squares.

Highlights of Almería's Old Town

- **Plaza Vieja:** The heart of the Old Town, this square is home to the **Almería City Hall and charming cafes**.
- **Casa de los Puche:** A beautifully preserved **Andalusian mansion** that offers a glimpse into **17th-century Spanish life**.
- **Arab Cisterns:** Hidden beneath the city, these ancient **water reservoirs** were built during **Moorish rule** to store water for the community.

The Soul of Almería

Exploring the Old Town is like peeling back **layers of history**, where **Moorish, Catholic, and Spanish traditions** blend seamlessly. It's the perfect place to **get lost in time, sip on traditional tapas, and experience the rhythm of local life**.

Chapter 4: Exploring Almería's Coastline

Almería's coastline is a **true Mediterranean gem**, offering a stunning blend of **golden beaches, rugged cliffs, and charming fishing villages**. With the warm waters of the **Mediterranean Sea** lapping against its shores, the province is a **paradise for beach lovers, water sports enthusiasts, and nature seekers alike**.

Unlike some of Spain's busier coastal destinations, Almería's beaches remain **pristine and unspoiled**, many of them nestled within the breathtaking landscapes of **Cabo de Gata-Níjar Natural Park**. Whether you're looking for a **quiet cove to escape the crowds, an adventure on the water, or a traditional seaside village to explore**, Almería's coastline has something special to offer.

In this chapter, we'll dive into:

- **The best beaches in Almería**, from the famous **Playa de los Genoveses** to the secluded shores of **Playa de los Muertos**.
- **Exciting water sports and activities**, including **diving, kayaking, and sailing**.
- **Charming coastal villages and hidden coves**, where time seems to slow down.

Let's set off on an unforgettable journey along **one of Spain's most spectacular coastlines!**

4.1 Best Beaches: Playa de los Genoveses, Playa de Mónsul, and More

When it comes to beaches, **Almería is a dream come true**. From vast, untouched stretches of sand to small, intimate coves, each beach has its own unique charm. Here are some of the most breathtaking spots to visit:

Playa de los Genoveses: A Slice of Paradise

Located within **Cabo de Gata-Níjar Natural Park**, **Playa de los Genoveses** is one of the most **pristine and untouched** beaches in Almería. This bay, with its **fine golden sand and calm turquoise waters**, is ideal for those seeking a peaceful, natural escape.

Why You'll Love It

 No high-rise hotels or developments—just pure, unspoiled nature.
 Shallow, gentle waves, making it perfect for swimming.
 Surrounded by rolling sand dunes and volcanic hills, creating a postcard-worthy landscape.

Playa de Mónsul: A Movie-Worthy Beach

Just a short distance from Playa de los Genoveses lies **Playa de Mónsul**, one of the most **iconic beaches in**

29

Spain. This spot is famous for its **dramatic volcanic rock formations**, which have served as a backdrop for films like *Indiana Jones and the Last Crusade*.

Highlights of Playa de Mónsul

- The **massive volcanic rock formation** in the middle of the beach, sculpted by time and nature.
- Crystal-clear waters, **ideal for snorkeling**.
- A wild, untouched atmosphere—**no beach bars or commercial establishments** in sight.

Playa de los Muertos: A Hidden Gem

Despite its slightly ominous name (which translates to *Beach of the Dead*), **Playa de los Muertos** is widely regarded as **one of the most beautiful beaches in Spain**. It features **sparkling blue waters, smooth white pebbles, and a stunningly clear seabed**.

 Getting There: Be prepared for a **steep but rewarding 20-minute walk** down to the beach.

Why Visit?

- **Some of the clearest waters in Almería**—ideal for snorkeling.
- A **sense of seclusion and tranquility**, perfect for a relaxing beach day.

More Stunning Beaches to Explore

- **Playa de las Negras** – A bohemian beach with laid-back vibes and charming beachfront cafés.
- **San José Beach** – A family-friendly spot with **soft sands and easy access to restaurants.**
- **Cala de Enmedio** – A **small, hidden cove with turquoise waters**, perfect for a quiet retreat.

4.2 Water Sports and Activities: Diving, Kayaking, and Sailing

Almería isn't just about **relaxing on the beach**—it's also a **fantastic destination for adventure seekers**! Thanks to its **clear waters, diverse marine life, and dramatic coastal landscapes**, it's a prime spot for **water sports and outdoor activities.**

Diving in Almería: Explore an Underwater Wonderland

The waters off Almería's coast are **a diver's paradise**, offering **hidden caves, vibrant reefs, and an array of marine species.**

Best Diving Spots

Cabo de Gata Marine Reserve – Home to **colorful coral, octopuses, and even seahorses.**
 Las Negras and El Playazo – Perfect for **beginner divers**, with **crystal-clear waters and gentle currents.**

Isla de San Andrés – A small island **teeming with marine biodiversity**, ideal for underwater photography.

Kayaking: Paddle Through Breathtaking Coves

Kayaking is **one of the best ways to explore Almería's rugged coastline**. With towering cliffs, hidden caves, and untouched beaches, a **kayak tour** offers a unique perspective of the **Mediterranean's natural beauty**.

Top Kayaking Routes

- **From San José to Playa de los Genoveses** – A scenic route with **spectacular rock formations**.
- **The Hidden Coves of Cabo de Gata** – Paddle into **secluded inlets and discover beaches accessible only by sea**.

Sailing and Boat Tours: Discover Almería from the Water

If you prefer to **relax while taking in the sights**, a **boat tour** is a fantastic option. Many companies offer **sunset cruises, dolphin-watching tours, and private charters** along the coast.

Why Try It?

- See **Almería's coastline from a new perspective**.

- Enjoy a **romantic sunset sail on the Mediterranean.**
- Spot **dolphins and other marine wildlife.**

4.3 Coastal Villages and Hidden Coves

Beyond the beaches, **Almería's coastal villages** offer a glimpse into **traditional Andalusian life**, with **whitewashed houses, picturesque harbors, and fresh seafood restaurants.**

Níjar: A Traditional Andalusian Gem

Located just **a short drive from the coast**, **Níjar** is a charming village known for its **craftsmanship, pottery, and beautiful mountain views.** Strolling through its **narrow streets**, you'll find **local artisans selling ceramics, rugs, and handmade jewelry.**

Las Negras: A Bohemian Beach Town

A laid-back village with a **hippie vibe**, **Las Negras** is perfect for those looking to experience **Almería's artistic and alternative side.** With **chilled-out beach bars, music festivals, and a vibrant expat community**, it's a **great place to unwind.**

Aguamarga: A Hidden Coastal Retreat

If you're seeking a **peaceful escape**, **Aguamarga** is a quiet fishing village with **pristine beaches, charming whitewashed houses, and excellent seafood restaurants**. It's the perfect place to **experience slow, coastal living**.

Chapter 5: Natural Wonders and Outdoor Adventures

Almería is a region of **stunning natural diversity**, where **volcanic cliffs meet the deep blue Mediterranean**, and **arid deserts stretch into rolling mountain ranges**. Unlike many other Spanish destinations known for their **urban landscapes and cultural heritage**, Almería captivates visitors with its **raw, untamed beauty**. From the **protected lands of Cabo de Gata-Níjar Natural Park** to the **otherworldly terrain of the Tabernas Desert**, this province is **a paradise for nature lovers and outdoor enthusiasts**.

In this chapter, we will explore:

- **Cabo de Gata-Níjar Natural Park**, one of Spain's most spectacular coastal reserves.
- **The Sierra Alhamilla mountains and the unique desert landscapes** that have served as filming locations for Hollywood classics.
- **Hiking and eco-tourism activities**, where you can immerse yourself in Almería's wild beauty.
- **The incredible birdwatching and wildlife experiences** that make this region a sanctuary for nature enthusiasts.

Let's begin our journey into **Almería's breathtaking outdoor wonders**!

5.1 Cabo de Gata-Níjar Natural Park

If there's one place in Almería that **truly embodies the region's natural splendor**, it's **Cabo de Gata-Níjar Natural Park**. Stretching along **more than 60 kilometers of coastline**, this **UNESCO Biosphere Reserve** is a haven for **pristine beaches, rugged cliffs, and diverse marine life**.

A Landscape of Volcanic Beauty

Cabo de Gata is **Spain's largest protected coastal area**, shaped by **ancient volcanic activity**. As you explore, you'll notice **dramatic rock formations, black lava flows, and hidden coves carved by the sea**. The landscape is **almost lunar-like**, with **reddish-brown mountains giving way to bright turquoise waters**.

Things to Do in Cabo de Gata

- **Hike to the Mirador de la Amatista** for **stunning panoramic views of the coastline**.
- **Visit Playa de los Muertos**, often ranked among **Spain's most beautiful beaches**.
- **Explore the salt flats of Las Salinas**, where flamingos and other migratory birds gather.

Exploring Cabo de Gata's Hidden Treasures

Beyond its **beaches and landscapes**, Cabo de Gata is dotted with **charming fishing villages** like **San José and La Isleta del Moro**, where you can enjoy **fresh seafood, laid-back atmospheres, and picture-perfect coastal views**.

If you're a fan of **snorkeling or diving**, head to **Los Escullos or Cala del Plomo**, where the **crystal-clear waters reveal vibrant marine life beneath the surface**.

5.2 Sierra Alhamilla and Desert Landscapes

While Almería's coastline is breathtaking, its **inland landscapes are equally impressive**. One of the most striking features is the **Sierra Alhamilla, a mountain range that rises above the arid desert plains**, offering an oasis of greenery amid the dry surroundings.

Sierra Alhamilla: An Oasis in the Desert

Located **just outside the city of Almería**, Sierra Alhamilla is a **refreshing escape from the coastal heat**. This area is home to **natural hot springs, scenic hiking trails, and ancient ruins**, making it a **perfect spot for outdoor enthusiasts**.

Why Visit Sierra Alhamilla?

Thermal Baths – Soak in the **natural hot springs of Baños de Sierra Alhamilla**, which have been used since **Roman times**.
 Incredible Views – Hike to the **highest points of the range** for panoramic vistas of the **desert below**.
 Diverse Wildlife – Spot **eagles, mountain goats, and rare Mediterranean plant species**.

The Tabernas Desert: Spain's Only True Desert

Just beyond the Sierra Alhamilla lies the **Tabernas Desert**, often called **"Europe's only true desert"**. This **otherworldly landscape** of **eroded rock formations, dry riverbeds, and vast open spaces** has been the setting for countless **Hollywood films, including famous spaghetti Westerns like** *The Good, the Bad, and the Ugly*.

What to Do in the Tabernas Desert

- **Visit the old film sets** at **Oasys MiniHollywood**, where classic Westerns were filmed.
- **Explore the unique rock formations** and canyons on a **guided 4x4 tour**.
- **Go stargazing**—the desert's **clear skies** make it one of the **best places in Spain for astrophotography**.

5.3 Hiking and Eco-Tourism Activities

For those who love **active outdoor adventures**, Almería offers some of **Spain's most rewarding hiking trails**. Whether you're trekking through **mountains, deserts, or coastal cliffs**, there's a path for everyone.

Top Hiking Trails in Almería

Ruta de las Amoladeras – A **scenic trail through Cabo de Gata**, offering breathtaking views of the Mediterranean.
El Cerrillo Redondo – A **moderate hike through the Sierra Alhamilla**, leading to ancient ruins and hot springs.
Desierto de Tabernas Route – A hike through the **otherworldly landscapes of the Tabernas Desert**, perfect for photography.

Sustainable Tourism and Eco-Friendly Adventures

Almería is committed to **eco-tourism**, with many local companies offering **sustainable tours** that focus on **preserving the natural environment**. Visitors can participate in **conservation efforts**, such as **reforestation programs** and **wildlife protection initiatives**.

Ways to Explore Sustainably

Join a guided eco-tour that emphasizes **respect for nature.**
Stay in an eco-friendly lodge near Cabo de Gata.
Follow "Leave No Trace" principles while hiking and camping.

5.4 Birdwatching and Wildlife Exploration

Almería is a **haven for birdwatchers and wildlife enthusiasts**, thanks to its **diverse ecosystems** that attract a wide variety of **migratory and resident species.**

Best Birdwatching Spots in Almería

Las Salinas de Cabo de Gata – A prime location for **flamingos, herons, and wading birds.**
Tabernas Desert – Home to **birds of prey, including golden eagles and peregrine falcons.**
Sierra María-Los Vélez Natural Park – A mountainous region where you can spot **griffon vultures and rare songbirds.**

Wildlife Encounters in Almería

Aside from birds, Almería is home to **a variety of fascinating wildlife**, including:

- **Iberian ibex**, often seen climbing rocky slopes.
- **Wild boars**, which roam the Sierra Alhamilla forests.
- **Chameleons**, hiding in the bushes of Cabo de Gata.

For a more immersive wildlife experience, consider joining a **guided nature tour**, where local experts can **help you spot rare and elusive species**.

Chapter 6: Almería's Unique Film Heritage

Almería's landscape is more than just a **natural wonder**—it's a **global cinematic treasure**. With its **dramatic deserts, rugged mountains, and unspoiled coastlines**, this region has served as the **backdrop for some of the most legendary films in Hollywood history**. From **spaghetti Westerns to epic blockbusters**, Almería's **striking scenery has transported audiences to the American Wild West, distant planets, and ancient civilizations**.

In this chapter, we will explore:

- **How Almería became the Hollywood of Europe**, attracting world-renowned directors and actors.
- **Famous movies filmed in Almería**, from Sergio Leone's Western classics to modern hits.
- **The Western theme parks**, where visitors can step into a real-life movie set.
- **Film tourism in Almería**, with exciting thematic tours that bring cinematic history to life.

Let's journey into **Almería's film legacy and uncover the magic of its silver screen history!**

6.1 How Almería Became the Hollywood of Europe

In the mid-20th century, Hollywood filmmakers stumbled upon **a hidden gem in southern Spain**—Almería. Its **unique blend of desert landscapes, coastal cliffs, and historic villages** made it the perfect substitute for locations ranging from **the American Wild West to the Middle East and even outer space.**

The Birth of Almería's Film Industry

The 1960s marked the beginning of **Almería's golden age in cinema**. During this period, Italian director **Sergio Leone** chose the **Tabernas Desert** as the setting for his iconic **spaghetti Westerns**, starring **Clint Eastwood**. These low-budget yet visually stunning films captured the **rugged beauty of Almería**, putting it on the international filmmaking map.

Why Did Hollywood Choose Almería?

A Desert in Europe – The Tabernas Desert is **Europe's only true desert**, making it the perfect stand-in for the American Southwest.
 Diverse Landscapes – From **coastal cliffs to rocky canyons**, Almería offers a wide range of natural settings.
 Sunny Weather – With **over 300 days of sunshine a year**, filming schedules were rarely interrupted.

Affordable Production Costs – Filming in Spain was significantly cheaper than shooting in the U.S. or Italy.

This combination of factors led to **hundreds of films being shot in Almería**, turning the province into **the Hollywood of Europe**.

6.2 Famous Movies Filmed in Almería

Over the decades, **Almería has hosted some of the most legendary movie productions**, featuring stars like **Clint Eastwood, Harrison Ford, Arnold Schwarzenegger, and even Sean Connery**.

The Spaghetti Western Era

Perhaps the most **iconic films associated with Almería** are the **spaghetti Westerns** of the 1960s and 1970s. These films, produced mainly by Italian directors, recreated the Wild West with **Almería's sun-scorched terrain and rustic villages**.

Famous Westerns Filmed in Almería

- **"The Good, the Bad, and the Ugly" (1966)** – One of the most famous Westerns of all time, directed by Sergio Leone and starring Clint Eastwood.

- **"A Fistful of Dollars" (1964)** – The movie that launched Clint Eastwood's career and introduced the world to the spaghetti Western.
- **"For a Few Dollars More" (1965)** – Another Sergio Leone masterpiece featuring **epic shootouts filmed in Almería's canyons and villages**.

Hollywood Blockbusters Filmed in Almería

As time went on, Almería's film industry expanded beyond Westerns, attracting major Hollywood productions. The region became the setting for **epic adventures, war films, and even sci-fi blockbusters**.

Notable Hollywood Films Shot in Almería

- **"Indiana Jones and the Last Crusade" (1989)** – Several scenes, including the journey to the desert temple, were filmed in the Tabernas Desert.
- **"Lawrence of Arabia" (1962)** – The Oscar-winning epic used Almería's landscapes to recreate the Arabian desert.
- **"Exodus: Gods and Kings" (2014)** – Directed by Ridley Scott, this biblical epic transformed Almería into ancient Egypt.
- **"Conan the Barbarian" (1982)** – Arnold Schwarzenegger roamed the Tabernas Desert in this sword-and-sorcery classic.

Even today, **modern filmmakers continue to choose Almería** as a backdrop, proving that its **cinematic charm is timeless**.

6.3 The Western Theme Parks: Oasys Mini Hollywood, Fort Bravo, and Texas Hollywood

To preserve Almería's **film legacy**, many of the original Western movie sets have been transformed into **theme parks and attractions**, allowing visitors to step back in time to the **glory days of the Wild West**.

Oasys Mini Hollywood

Originally built as a set for **spaghetti Westerns**, Oasys Mini Hollywood is now a fully functioning **Western-themed park**. Visitors can explore **authentic saloons, a sheriff's office, and a Wild West bank**, just like in the old movies.

Top Attractions at Oasys Mini Hollywood

- **Live Wild West shows**, complete with **staged gunfights and cowboy duels**.
- **A small zoo**, home to exotic animals.
- **Costume dress-ups**, where visitors can **become cowboys or outlaws for the day**.

Fort Bravo

Located in the **heart of the Tabernas Desert**, Fort Bravo was another major film set for Westerns. It remains one of **the best-preserved Western towns** in Spain.

Why Visit Fort Bravo?

- **Explore real Western movie sets**, unchanged since their Hollywood days.
- **Take a horseback ride through the desert**, just like a cowboy.
- **Watch action-packed stunt shows**, bringing Western legends to life.

Texas Hollywood (Western Leone)

This is one of the few places where **movies are still filmed today**. Many modern productions use Texas Hollywood as a location, keeping Almería's film tradition alive.

Visitors can **wander through a dusty Western town**, watch **exciting reenactments**, and even **meet actors in full cowboy gear**.

6.4 Film Tourism and Thematic Tours

Almería's **film heritage has inspired a growing number of cinematic tours**, allowing visitors to relive the magic of the movies.

Popular Film Tourism Experiences

- **Guided movie location tours** – Explore famous filming spots from classics like *Indiana Jones* and *The Good, the Bad, and the Ugly*.
- **Film festivals and events** – Almería hosts **an annual Western Film Festival**, celebrating its movie-making legacy.
- **Cinematic experiences** – Try **Western-style horseback riding** or spend the night in an old-fashioned saloon.

For die-hard movie fans, there's **no better way to experience Almería than by stepping onto the very sets where legends were made**.

Chapter 7: Gastronomy and Local Cuisine

Almería's cuisine is a **true reflection of its diverse history, coastal setting, and agricultural richness.** Situated in **Andalusia**, this province boasts a gastronomic culture that blends **Moorish influences, Mediterranean flavors, and Spanish traditions.** Whether you're indulging in a bowl of **gurullos con conejo (traditional rabbit stew)**, savoring fresh **grilled seafood**, or hopping from one **tapas bar** to another, Almería offers a **culinary journey full of rich flavors and local character.**

In this chapter, we'll explore:

- **Traditional Almerían dishes**, packed with local ingredients and centuries-old recipes.
- **The best tapas bars**, where you can experience the unique tradition of **free tapas**.
- **Seafood specialties**, highlighting Almería's close connection to the Mediterranean.
- **Food markets and dining experiences**, where visitors can immerse themselves in the region's culinary culture.

Get ready to **discover the soul of Almería through its food!**

7.1 Traditional Almerían Dishes

A Taste of Almería's Heritage

Almería's cuisine has been shaped by its **history, geography, and culture**. The **Moors**, who ruled the region for centuries, left a lasting mark on the local diet, introducing **spices, almonds, saffron, and honey**. Meanwhile, the province's **coastal waters** provide fresh fish and seafood, while its **fertile lands** yield some of the best produce in Spain.

Below are some of the **most iconic dishes you must try** when visiting Almería:

Gurullos con Conejo (Rabbit and Pasta Stew)

A true **Almerían classic**, this hearty dish consists of **small, handmade pasta pieces (gurullos)** cooked with **rabbit, bell peppers, tomatoes, and saffron**. The result is a **rich, flavorful stew** that perfectly represents the **rustic and traditional** flavors of the region.

Ajo Colorao (Red Garlic Stew)

This dish, popular in **coastal towns**, is a **thick, red-hued stew** made from **potatoes, salt cod, red peppers, garlic, and olive oil**. It has a **delicate balance of smoky and savory flavors**, making it a must-try for seafood lovers.

Patatas a lo Pobre (Poor Man's Potatoes)

Despite its humble origins, this dish is **packed with flavor**. Thinly sliced **potatoes are slowly fried with green peppers, onions, and garlic**, creating a **soft and golden delight** that is often served with **fried eggs or grilled meats**.

Almería's Moorish-Inspired Sweets

Thanks to its **Moorish past**, Almería boasts a variety of delicious desserts influenced by Arabic cuisine. Look out for:

- **Tortas de Chicharrones** – A pastry made with lard and sugar, often enjoyed with coffee.
- **Roscos de Anís** – Anise-flavored ring-shaped pastries.
- **Mantecados and Polvorones** – Traditional Andalusian almond shortbreads, especially popular during Christmas.

These **traditional dishes tell the story of Almería's history and people**, making them essential for any visitor looking to experience the local culture.

7.2 The Best Tapas Bars in Almería

The Unique Tradition of Free Tapas

One of the **most exciting aspects of dining in Almería** is the **time-honored tradition of free tapas**. Unlike many other parts of Spain, where you pay separately for tapas, Almería is famous for serving a **free tapa with every drink ordered**. This means that a simple **beer or glass of wine** can turn into a **full meal** if you choose wisely!

Below are some of **the best tapas bars** in Almería that you shouldn't miss:

Casa Puga

Location: Historic Old Town
 Must-Try: Gambas al Ajillo (Garlic Shrimp), Jamón Ibérico

A legendary spot, **Casa Puga** has been serving tapas since **1870**. Its **classic wooden interior** and **hanging jamón legs** create the perfect setting for an authentic tapas experience.

 La Mala

Location: Near the Cathedral
  Must-Try: Pulpo a la Gallega (Galician-Style Octopus), Goat Cheese with Honey

For a **modern twist on tapas**, La Mala offers **creative and gourmet-style small plates** in a vibrant atmosphere.

El Quinto Toro

Location: Plaza de las Flores
Must-Try: Carrillada (Braised Pork Cheeks), Albóndigas en Salsa (Meatballs in Sauce)

A great choice for **meat lovers**, this bar serves **generous portions of hearty Andalusian favorites**.

Exploring **Almería's tapas scene** is an adventure in itself, and hopping from one bar to another is the **best way to taste a little bit of everything**.

7.3 Seafood and Coastal Culinary Delights

Being a **coastal city**, Almería is a **paradise for seafood lovers**. The **Mediterranean waters** provide an abundance of **fresh fish, squid, shrimp, and shellfish**, which are expertly prepared in local kitchens.

Must-Try Seafood Dishes

- **Espetos de Sardinas** – Sardines skewered and grilled over an open flame, best enjoyed with a sea view.
- **Calamares a la Andaluza** – Lightly battered and fried squid, a crispy and tender delicacy.
- **Arroz a Banda** – A rice dish cooked in rich fish broth, often served with aioli.

- **Gambas Rojas de Garrucha** – The famous **red prawns from Garrucha**, considered some of the best in Spain.

For the **best seafood experience**, visit the **coastal fishing villages** near Almería, where you'll find **seaside restaurants serving the freshest catches of the day**.

7.4 Food Markets and Authentic Dining Experiences

Mercado Central de Almería

Location: Calle Aguilar de Campoo
 Why Visit?

Almería's **Mercado Central** is the best place to **experience the city's local produce, seafood, and artisanal products**. Walk through the market and see **fresh fish, colorful fruits, and regional cheeses**, all while soaking in the **bustling atmosphere**.

Farm-to-Table Experiences

Almería is also famous for its **greenhouses**, which produce **a large percentage of Europe's fruits and vegetables**. Some local restaurants focus on **farm-to-table dining**, using **organic, locally sourced ingredients** to craft **delicious and sustainable meals**.

Wine and Gastronomic Tours

To fully appreciate Almería's culinary scene, consider joining a **food and wine tour**. These experiences take you to:

- **Olive oil farms**, where you can taste some of Spain's finest extra virgin olive oil.
- **Vineyards**, where local wines are paired with traditional tapas.
- **Rural family-run restaurants**, where age-old recipes are still prepared with love.

Chapter 8: Wine and Local Beverages

Almería is not just a destination for **stunning landscapes, rich history, and incredible food**—it is also home to a **diverse selection of wines and traditional beverages** that reflect the region's **Mediterranean charm**. While Almería may not be as internationally recognized as other Spanish wine regions like **La Rioja or Ribera del Duero**, it has a **growing reputation for producing high-quality wines**, thanks to its **unique climate, rich soil, and innovative winemakers**.

Beyond wine, Almería also boasts **a variety of local drinks**, including **traditional liqueurs, craft beers, and refreshing non-alcoholic options**. Another essential part of the region's gastronomy is **olive oil**, often considered "liquid gold" due to its superior quality and deep-rooted importance in Andalusian cuisine.

In this chapter, we will explore:

- The **wine regions of Almería**, their history, and their unique characteristics.
- The best **bodegas (wineries)** to visit for an unforgettable **wine-tasting experience**.
- **Traditional beverages**, from **local spirits to refreshing summer drinks**.

- The **importance of olive oil and other regional specialties**, essential to Almerían gastronomy.

8.1 The Wine Regions of Almería

A Unique Winemaking Heritage

Almería's **winemaking tradition dates back centuries**, with evidence of grape cultivation during the times of the **Phoenicians and Romans**. However, it was during the **Moorish period** that the region truly developed sophisticated **agricultural techniques,** many of which still influence winemaking today.

Despite being a relatively **dry and arid province,** Almería has **microclimates** that allow for the production of **diverse and high-quality wines**. From the **mountainous vineyards of the Alpujarra** to the **coastal plains**, each area brings its own **distinct character to the wines produced there.**

Main Wine-Producing Areas in Almería

1. **Laujar-Alpujarra**

    - This is **Almería's most renowned wine region**, located in the **foothills of the Sierra Nevada**.

- The altitude and cooler temperatures allow for the production of **balanced, aromatic wines**.
- Varieties: **Tempranillo, Garnacha, Macabeo, and Syrah**.

2. **Desierto de Tabernas**

    - Known as **Europe's only desert wine region**, this area benefits from a **unique combination of sun exposure and mineral-rich soil**.
    - The dry climate produces **robust, full-bodied red wines**.
    - Varieties: **Cabernet Sauvignon, Merlot, and Chardonnay**.

3. **Vélez-Rubio and Vélez-Blanco**

    - Located in **northern Almería**, this region is home to small family-run wineries.
    - Known for **organic and natural winemaking methods**.
    - Varieties: **Monastrell, Moscatel, and Pedro Ximénez**.

Thanks to a **resurgence in boutique wineries and organic vineyards**, Almería's wines are **gaining recognition for their bold flavors, rich textures, and deep connection to the land**.

8.2 Bodegas and Wine Tasting Experiences

A visit to Almería would not be complete without experiencing a **wine-tasting tour at one of its charming bodegas**. Many of these wineries offer **guided tours**, where visitors can **learn about the production process, stroll through picturesque vineyards, and, of course, sample some incredible wines**.

Top Wineries to Visit in Almería

1. **Bodega Fuente Victoria (Laujar-Alpujarra)**

    - A **family-run winery** known for its **organic wines and scenic vineyard views**.
    - Offers **intimate tastings** paired with local cheeses and cured meats.
2. **Bodega Cortijo El Cura (Laujar-Alpujarra)**

    - One of Almería's **pioneers in ecological winemaking**.
    - Specializes in **natural wines** with **minimal intervention**.
3. **Bodegas Perfer (Desierto de Tabernas)**

    - Known for **bold red wines** that reflect the **dry desert terroir**.

- Offers **jeep tours through the vineyards**, followed by **tastings in a rustic cellar**.
4. **Bodega Palomillo (Vélez-Rubio)**

    - A hidden gem focusing on **artisanal winemaking**.
    - Provides **wine and tapas pairings**, allowing visitors to enjoy the **full Almerían experience**.

A **wine tour in Almería** is not just about tasting—it's about **immersing yourself in the land, learning from passionate winemakers, and experiencing the true flavors of Andalusia**.

8.3 Traditional Drinks of the Region

While wine is undoubtedly a highlight, Almería is also home to **unique beverages** that locals have enjoyed for centuries.

Local Liqueurs and Spirits

- **Anís de Almería** – A sweet and aromatic **anise-flavored liqueur**, commonly sipped as a digestive.

- **Mistela** – A traditional Andalusian drink made by **mixing grape must with brandy**, resulting in a **sweet, fortified wine.**
- **Ron Pálido** – A **light rum distilled in the region**, often enjoyed neat or in cocktails.

Refreshing Summer Drinks

- **Tinto de Verano** – A **refreshing mix of red wine and soda**, perfect for warm Almería afternoons.
- **Rebujito** – A **popular Andalusian cocktail** made with **sherry and lemon-lime soda**, often enjoyed at festivals.
- **Café Asiático** – A **unique Almerían coffee cocktail** made with espresso, condensed milk, and a touch of **brandy and cinnamon.**

These drinks **offer a glimpse into Almería's culture and traditions**, making them an essential part of any visit.

8.4 Olive Oil and Other Local Specialties

The Importance of Olive Oil in Almería

Almería is home to **some of the finest olive oils in Spain**, thanks to its **ideal growing conditions and centuries-old production methods**. Olive oil is **a**

cornerstone of Andalusian cuisine, used in everything from **simple tapas to elaborate stews**.

Best Olive Oils to Try

1. **Oro del Desierto** – A multi-award-winning olive oil produced in **Tabernas**, known for its **smooth, fruity taste**.
2. **Castillo de Tabernas** – Offers **high-quality extra virgin olive oil** with **notes of almond and green apple**.
3. **Finca la Torre** – A premium organic olive oil with a **peppery finish**.

Visiting an **olive oil farm** in Almería allows you to **learn about traditional pressing methods, sample different varieties, and appreciate why this "liquid gold" is so prized**.

Other Regional Specialties

- **Almonds and Honey** – Inspired by Moorish traditions, these ingredients are widely used in **desserts and pastries**.
- **Cured Meats and Cheeses** – Try **Jamón Serrano and goat cheeses** from the region's rural farms.
- **Locally Grown Fruits and Vegetables** – Thanks to its **greenhouses, Almería is known as the "Garden of Europe"**, producing

tomatoes, peppers, and melons of the highest quality.

Chapter 9: Cultural Events and Festivals

Almería is more than just a place of **stunning coastal landscapes and historic landmarks**—it is a city that beats to the rhythm of its **vibrant cultural traditions and festivals**. Throughout the year, locals and visitors alike immerse themselves in a wide range of **celebrations that bring the city to life**, from deeply spiritual processions during **Semana Santa** to the colorful spectacle of the **Feria de Almería**.

Music, dance, and art also play a crucial role in the region's identity, with an array of **music festivals, flamenco performances, and art exhibitions** filling the streets with creative energy. Beyond the grand celebrations, **local traditions and folklore** remain an essential part of Almerían culture, passed down through generations.

In this chapter, we will explore:

- The **deeply moving Semana Santa celebrations**, one of Spain's most famous religious traditions.
- The **joyful Feria de Almería**, where the city explodes with color, music, and festivity.
- The **best music and art festivals**, showcasing the city's artistic and creative spirit.

- The **enduring traditions and folklore** that make Almería a truly unique cultural destination.

Let's dive into the heartbeat of Almería's cultural scene.

9.1 Semana Santa and Religious Celebrations

The Sacred Week in Almería

Semana Santa (Holy Week) is one of the **most significant religious and cultural events** in Almería, as it is in the rest of Andalusia. Taking place during the week leading up to **Easter Sunday**, this centuries-old tradition brings together **faith, artistry, and solemnity** in an extraordinary display of devotion.

The celebration is marked by **impressive processions**, where **brotherhoods (cofradías)**, dressed in traditional robes and tall pointed hoods, carry **ornate religious floats (pasos)** through the streets. These pasos, often weighing several tons, are **masterpieces of religious sculpture**, depicting **scenes from the Passion of Christ** or images of the **Virgin Mary**.

Key Processions in Almería

Each night during Semana Santa, different processions take place, **each with its own unique atmosphere and significance.** Some of the most notable include:

- **Domingo de Ramos (Palm Sunday): La Borriquita** – A lively and family-friendly procession marking **Jesus' arrival in Jerusalem**.
- **Jueves Santo (Holy Thursday): El Silencio** – One of the most **awe-inspiring processions**, where the city falls into complete silence as the pasos make their way through the streets by candlelight.
- **Viernes Santo (Good Friday): El Santo Sepulcro** – A deeply solemn and emotional procession that symbolizes the **burial of Christ**.
- **Domingo de Resurrección (Easter Sunday): Jesús Resucitado** – A joyful and triumphant procession that **celebrates the resurrection** with music and flowers.

The Atmosphere of Semana Santa

Even for non-religious visitors, **Semana Santa is an unforgettable experience**. The air is filled with **the scent of incense**, the sound of **marching bands and mournful saetas (flamenco-style hymns)**, and the sight of thousands of spectators watching **in reverence and admiration**. It is a time of **reflection, tradition, and intense emotions**, showcasing Almería's deep spiritual roots.

9.2 Feria de Almería: The Grand Annual Festival

A Celebration of Joy and Tradition

If Semana Santa represents **Almería's solemn side**, the **Feria de Almería** is its **most exuberant and colorful celebration**. Held every **August**, this week-long festival is a time when **the entire city comes alive with music, dancing, food, and festivities**.

The Feria dates back to **1805**, originally established to commemorate **the patron saint of Almería, the Virgen del Mar**. Over the centuries, it has evolved into **one of the most anticipated events of the year**, drawing visitors from all over Spain.

What to Expect at the Feria

1. **The Grand Parade and Fireworks**

    - The **Feria officially begins** with a **spectacular parade and fireworks display**, setting the stage for a week of excitement.

2. **The Fairground (Recinto Ferial)**

    - Located on the outskirts of the city, this **huge fairground** is packed with **rides, food stalls, and traditional casetas (pavilions)** where locals dance **sevillanas** late into the night.

3. **Flamenco and Live Music**

- One of the highlights of the Feria is the **flamenco performances**, with some of **Andalusia's best dancers and musicians** taking the stage.
4. **Bullfighting Events**
    - While controversial, bullfighting remains a **traditional part of the Feria**, held at Almería's historic **Plaza de Toros**.
5. **The Feria del Mediodía (Midday Fair)**
    - During the day, the streets of **Almería's historic center** become a massive open-air party, with bars and restaurants serving **tapas, drinks, and local specialties**.

The **Feria de Almería is a time for pure joy and festivity**, where locals and visitors come together to **celebrate life, dance, eat, and create unforgettable memories**.

9.3 Music and Art Festivals

Beyond its traditional festivals, Almería is also home to a **thriving music and arts scene**, with numerous events that attract **artists, musicians, and performers** from all over Spain and beyond.

Top Music and Arts Festivals in Almería

1. **Almería Flamenca**

    o A festival dedicated to the **passionate and soulful art of flamenco**, featuring some of Spain's most talented dancers and musicians.
2. **Dreambeach Villaricos**

    o One of Spain's largest **electronic music festivals**, held on the beaches near Almería.
3. **Festival de Jazz de Almería**

    o A must-visit for jazz lovers, this festival brings together **international and Spanish jazz musicians** for incredible performances.
4. **FICAL (Festival Internacional de Cine de Almería)**

    o A celebration of **Almería's film heritage**, featuring **film screenings, guest speakers, and workshops**.

These festivals **showcase Almería's artistic spirit**, blending **traditional Andalusian culture with modern creativity**.

9.4 Local Traditions and Folklore

Beyond the major festivals, Almería's **local traditions and folklore** provide a fascinating glimpse into its **rich cultural heritage**.

Unique Local Traditions

- **The Virgen del Mar Pilgrimage** – A religious procession in honor of **Almería's patron saint**, featuring **boat parades and coastal celebrations**.
- **Night of San Juan (Noche de San Juan)** – A **midsummer festival** where locals gather on the beaches to **light bonfires, swim at midnight, and welcome the summer solstice**.
- **La Semana de la Tapa** – A celebration of **Almería's rich culinary heritage**, where restaurants and bars offer **special tapas menus**.

Folklore and Legends

- **The Legend of the Alcazaba Ghost** – Local tales speak of a **mysterious figure** roaming the **Alcazaba Fortress at night**.
- **The Gold of Rodalquilar** – Stories of **hidden treasures buried in the desert** still capture the imagination of treasure hunters today.

These traditions and stories **add depth to Almería's cultural identity**, keeping **the past alive in the hearts of its people**.

Chapter 10: Shopping and Handicrafts in Almería

Shopping in Almería is not just about buying things—it's about **experiencing the essence of Andalusian culture** through its local markets, traditional crafts, and modern boutiques. Whether you're wandering through **historic streets lined with artisan shops,** exploring **bustling local markets,** or seeking out **authentic souvenirs,** Almería offers a diverse shopping experience.

From **handcrafted ceramics and textiles** to **fresh local produce and high-end boutiques**, every corner of the city presents an opportunity to take home a piece of its charm. In this chapter, we'll uncover:

- The **best shopping streets and local markets**, where you'll find everything from fresh food to unique artisan goods.
- The **rich traditions of Almería's handicrafts**, including ceramics, pottery, and textiles.
- The **best places to buy authentic souvenirs**, ensuring you take home a true piece of Almería.
- The **modern shopping malls and designer boutiques** for those looking for a contemporary retail experience.

Let's dive into the **vibrant shopping scene** of Almería!

10.1 Best Shopping Streets and Local Markets

One of the best ways to **immerse yourself in Almería's local culture** is by strolling through its **lively shopping streets and traditional markets**. Here, locals and visitors alike enjoy **browsing stalls filled with fresh produce, artisanal crafts, and unique souvenirs**.

Calle de las Tiendas: Almería's Historic Shopping Street

The name of this street translates to **"Street of Shops"**, and it has been a shopping hub since the **Moorish era**. Located in the heart of the **Old Town**, Calle de las Tiendas is a **narrow, picturesque street lined with charming boutiques, artisan workshops, and traditional craft stores**.

What you'll find:

- **Handcrafted jewelry and accessories** made by local artisans.
- **Leather goods**, including belts, handbags, and shoes.
- **Traditional Andalusian clothing**, such as embroidered shawls and flamenco dresses.

Mercado Central de Almería: A Feast for the Senses

For a **true local shopping experience**, head to the **Mercado Central de Almería**. This historic market, dating back to the **19th century**, is the perfect place to **taste the flavors of Almería** while admiring its bustling atmosphere.

What you'll find:

- **Fresh seafood**, caught daily from the Mediterranean.
- **Olives, cheeses, and cured meats**, perfect for a picnic or to take home.
- **Locally grown fruits and vegetables**, known for their exceptional quality.

Visiting the market is not just about shopping—it's about **experiencing the sights, sounds, and aromas** of daily life in Almería.

Other Notable Markets in Almería

- **Mercadillo de los Martes (Tuesday Market)** – A weekly outdoor market selling **clothing, shoes, fresh produce, and household items**.
- **Almería's Flea Market (Rastro de Almería)** – A treasure trove of **antiques, second-hand books, and vintage finds**.

For those who love **street markets and vibrant local shopping**, Almería offers a **diverse and exciting array of options**.

10.2 Traditional Crafts: Ceramics, Pottery, and Textiles

Almería is a city with **a deep-rooted artisan culture**, where traditional crafts have been passed down **through generations**. From **Moorish-inspired ceramics** to **handwoven textiles**, the province is home to some of **Spain's most exquisite craftsmanship**.

Ceramics and Pottery: A Legacy of the Moors

The influence of **Al-Andalus** is still visible in Almería's ceramics, which feature **intricate geometric designs and vibrant colors**.

- Where to Buy:
    - **Sorbas** – A small town near Almería, famous for its **handmade pottery and traditional ceramic workshops**.
    - **Artisan shops in the Old Town** – Many sell **hand-painted ceramic plates, bowls, and tiles**, perfect for souvenirs.
- What to Look For:

- **Fajalauza-style pottery**, characterized by **blue and green floral designs on a white background.**
- **Hand-painted tiles**, often featuring **Andalusian motifs and Arabic calligraphy.**

Textiles and Embroidery: Andalusian Elegance

Almería has a long tradition of textile production, influenced by both **Moorish and Spanish styles**.

- **Where to Buy:**

    - **Local artisan workshops** – Specializing in **handwoven shawls, blankets, and traditional Andalusian fabrics.**
    - **Flamenco dress shops** – Selling **intricately embroidered dresses and accessories.**
- **What to Look For:**

    - **Rebujitos and mantones (shawls and scarves)**, often featuring **vibrant floral embroidery.**
    - **Handmade lace and crochet items**, showcasing **Spanish craftsmanship.**

Almería's traditional crafts **connect the past with the present**, allowing visitors to take home **a unique and meaningful piece of Andalusian history.**

10.3 Where to Buy Authentic Souvenirs

Finding the perfect souvenir can be challenging, but **Almería offers plenty of authentic and meaningful options**. Instead of mass-produced trinkets, why not take home something truly special?

Top Souvenirs to Buy in Almería

1. **Hand-Painted Ceramics** – Beautifully decorated plates, vases, and tiles.
2. **Olive Oil** – Some of Spain's finest extra virgin olive oil comes from Almería.
3. **Locally Made Wines** – A taste of the region's rich viticulture.
4. **Almerían Spices** – Paprika, saffron, and Mediterranean herbs.
5. **Leather Goods** – Handcrafted handbags, wallets, and belts.

Where to Find the Best Souvenirs

- **Calle de las Tiendas** – A historic street full of artisan shops.
- **Local markets** – Ideal for food-related souvenirs like olive oil and spices.
- **Specialty craft stores in Sorbas** – The best place for ceramics and pottery.

By choosing **authentic, locally made souvenirs**, you not only take home **a special memory of Almería**, but you also **support local artisans and businesses**.

10.4 Modern Shopping Malls and Boutiques

For those who enjoy **modern shopping experiences**, Almería also offers a selection of **contemporary shopping malls and high-end boutiques**.

Top Shopping Malls in Almería

1. **Centro Comercial Mediterráneo**

    - Almería's largest mall, featuring **international brands, fashion stores, and a cinema**.
    - Perfect for **mainstream retail shopping**.

2. **Torre Cárdenas Shopping Center**

    - A newer mall with **a wide range of shops, restaurants, and entertainment options**.
    - Ideal for those looking for **luxury brands and high-street fashion**.

3. **Gran Plaza in Roquetas de Mar**

- Located just outside Almería, offering **big-brand stores and department stores**.

Boutique Shopping in Almería

For a more **personalized and stylish shopping experience**, Almería's boutique stores offer **unique fashion, accessories, and home décor**. Some of the best areas for boutique shopping include:

- **Paseo de Almería** – The city's main shopping avenue, lined with **designer stores and elegant boutiques**.
- **Alcazaba District** – A charming area with **independent shops selling handmade goods and stylish clothing**.

Chapter 11: Day Trips and Excursions

Almería is a destination filled with **diverse landscapes, historic villages, and breathtaking coastlines**, making it the perfect base for **unforgettable day trips**. Whether you're looking for **charming whitewashed villages, golden beaches, dramatic desert landscapes, or mountain retreats**, the province offers a variety of excursions that cater to every traveler's taste.

In this chapter, we'll explore some of the most rewarding day trips from Almería, including:

- **Mojácar**, a picturesque **hilltop village** with a rich Moorish history.
- **Roquetas de Mar**, a vibrant **seaside resort town** known for its beaches and seafood.
- **Tabernas Desert**, a unique **semi-arid landscape** famous for its role in Spaghetti Western films.
- **Alpujarra Almeriense**, a **scenic mountain region** dotted with traditional villages and stunning natural beauty.

Each of these destinations offers **a unique glimpse into Almería's culture, history, and breathtaking**

landscapes, ensuring that your journey through the region is nothing short of extraordinary.

11.1 Mojácar: The Whitewashed Village on the Hills

Mojácar is one of the **most stunning villages in Almería**, perched on a **hilltop overlooking the Mediterranean Sea**. With its **whitewashed buildings, winding cobbled streets, and breathtaking coastal views**, Mojácar feels like a **storybook setting frozen in time**.

A Glimpse into Mojácar's History

Mojácar's origins date back to **Phoenician and Roman times**, but it was during the **Moorish era** that the village developed its distinctive **architecture and character**. The **white cubic houses, narrow alleyways, and decorative iron balconies** all bear the hallmarks of **Andalusian and Arabic influences**.

Top Attractions in Mojácar

- **Plaza Nueva** – The heart of the village, offering **panoramic views of the surrounding mountains and sea**.
- **Mirador del Castillo** – A scenic viewpoint at the highest point of Mojácar, perfect for capturing stunning photographs.

- **Iglesia de Santa María** – A **historic church** originally built as a mosque during the **Moorish rule**.
- **Fuente Mora** – A legendary fountain believed to be the **site of Mojácar's last Moorish surrender** in the 15th century.

Mojácar Playa: The Coastal Escape

Just **a few kilometers from the village**, Mojácar Playa offers **17 kilometers of golden beaches**, beachside bars, and **crystal-clear waters**. Whether you want to relax on the sand, swim in the Mediterranean, or enjoy a seafood meal by the sea, Mojácar Playa is an ideal retreat.

11.2 Roquetas de Mar: A Coastal Getaway

Roquetas de Mar is one of Almería's most popular **coastal towns**, known for its **sandy beaches, vibrant nightlife, and delicious seafood**. It is a **top destination for both relaxation and adventure**, making it an excellent day trip from Almería.

Beaches and Water Activities

- **Playa Serena** – One of the most famous beaches, offering **fine sand, gentle waves, and excellent facilities**.

- **Playa de Aguadulce** – A scenic **beach with a lively promenade**, filled with restaurants and bars.
- **Kayaking and Snorkeling** – Roquetas de Mar is **perfect for water sports**, with plenty of rental options available.

Exploring the Town

- **Castillo de Santa Ana** – A **beautifully restored 17th-century fortress**, offering panoramic sea views.
- **Punta Entinas-Sabinar Natural Reserve** – A **protected coastal area** home to flamingos, migratory birds, and salt marshes.
- **Puerto Deportivo** – The town's **charming marina**, lined with **cafés and seafood restaurants**.

Roquetas de Mar is a **seaside paradise**, combining the **beauty of Andalusian beaches** with a **rich cultural atmosphere**.

11.3 Tabernas Desert and its Western Film Sets

The **Tabernas Desert** is one of the **most fascinating landscapes in Spain**—a **barren, sun-scorched terrain reminiscent of the American Wild West**. This desert, often called **"Europe's only desert,"** is famous for its **dramatic rock formations, arid beauty, and legendary film sets**.

A Natural Wonder

The **Tabernas Desert** is a **protected natural area**, offering stunning views of **eroded rock formations, deep ravines, and endless sand dunes**. The desert's surreal beauty has made it a prime filming location for **Spaghetti Westerns, Hollywood blockbusters, and even Game of Thrones**.

Western-Themed Parks and Film Locations

- **Oasys Mini Hollywood** – Originally built as a movie set for **The Good, The Bad, and The Ugly**, this Western town has been transformed into a **theme park**, complete with live cowboy shows, a zoo, and film memorabilia.
- **Fort Bravo Texas Hollywood** – A fully functional **Western village**, where you can walk through saloons, watch stunt shows, and experience the atmosphere of the **Wild West**.
- **Western Leone** – A smaller but **authentic movie set**, built for **Sergio Leone's classic Western films**.

For film lovers and adventure seekers, the **Tabernas Desert is an unforgettable destination**, offering **Hollywood history in the heart of Andalusia**.

11.4 Exploring Alpujarra Almeriense

The **Alpujarra Almeriense** is a breathtaking region of **picturesque villages, rolling hills, and lush valleys** nestled in the **foothills of the Sierra Nevada Mountains**. This area, known for its **tranquility, traditional charm, and stunning landscapes**, offers a perfect escape from city life.

Charming Villages of the Alpujarra

- **Laujar de Andarax** – The largest town in the region, famous for its **vineyards, olive groves, and historic churches**.
- **Fondón** – A **quaint mountain village**, known for its **whitewashed houses and local wine production**.
- **Padules** – Home to the **Padules Ravine**, a stunning **natural swimming spot surrounded by rock formations**.

Hiking and Nature Activities

The Alpujarra Almeriense is a **paradise for outdoor enthusiasts**, offering:

- **Scenic hiking trails** through the **Sierra Nevada foothills**.

- **River walks** along **crystal-clear mountain streams**.
- **Wine-tasting tours** at family-run bodegas.

Whether you're exploring **historic villages, hiking through scenic landscapes, or sampling local delicacies**, the Alpujarra Almeriense is a **hidden gem worth discovering**.

Chapter 12: Nightlife and Entertainment

Almería may be known for its **sun-drenched beaches and historical landmarks**, but when the sun sets, the city transforms into a vibrant **hub of nightlife and entertainment**. Whether you're in the mood for a **chilled-out evening with tapas and wine, a high-energy dance floor, an intimate flamenco show, or an open-air cinema experience under the stars**, Almería offers something for every kind of night owl.

In this chapter, we'll explore:

- **The best bars and nightclubs** where locals and visitors come together to celebrate the night.
- **Traditional flamenco shows and live music venues** that capture the spirit of Andalusia.
- **Open-air cinemas and cultural performances** that make nightlife in Almería unique.
- **The late-night tapas culture**, an essential part of the city's social and culinary scene.

Whether you're looking for an unforgettable **party experience, an authentic cultural night out, or a laid-back evening filled with good food and conversation**, Almería has it all.

12.1 Best Bars and Nightclubs in Almería

Almería's nightlife is a mix of **trendy bars, beachside chiringuitos (beach bars), and high-energy nightclubs** that keep the city alive until the early morning hours. Whether you prefer sipping on a **craft cocktail in a stylish lounge**, dancing the night away in a **lively club**, or enjoying a **beer by the sea**, there's a spot in Almería for you.

Best Bars in Almería for a Relaxed Night Out

- **Casa Puga** – One of the **oldest and most famous taverns** in Almería, serving traditional Andalusian wines and tapas in a historic setting.
- **La Consentida** – A stylish cocktail bar with a chic atmosphere, perfect for a **romantic date night** or a **laid-back evening with friends**.
- **La Fuga** – Known for its **artsy and bohemian vibes**, this bar is a favorite among locals looking for an **alternative nightlife experience**.
- **Chaman Beach Club** – Located just outside the city, this **beachside bar** offers a fantastic mix of **cocktails, DJs, and sunset views over the Mediterranean**.

Best Nightclubs in Almería for Dancing and Partying

- **Mauka Club** – A **modern nightclub** with international DJs, neon lights, and a **high-energy dance floor**.
- **Mandala Beach Club** – Located in nearby Mojácar, this club **blends the beach with a party atmosphere**, offering live DJs and a VIP section.
- **Discoteca Kopa** – One of the city's **most popular late-night clubs**, playing a mix of **reggaeton, Latin, and electronic music**.

Whether you're looking for a casual drink or a **full-blown party**, Almería's nightlife scene has a diverse range of options.

12.2 Flamenco Shows and Live Music Venues

No trip to Almería is complete without experiencing **flamenco**, the passionate and soulful **Andalusian art form** that combines **singing, guitar playing, and expressive dance**. The city offers **intimate flamenco performances in traditional tablaos**, as well as lively bars featuring **live music spanning jazz, rock, and Latin rhythms**.

Where to Experience Authentic Flamenco in Almería

- **Peña El Taranto** – One of the **most respected flamenco clubs** in Andalusia, where talented performers bring **raw emotion and fiery footwork** to the stage.
- **La Guajira** – A small but **intensely atmospheric venue** that hosts **intimate flamenco nights and fusion music performances**.
- **Cueva de Roque** – A **cave-style flamenco venue** offering **dinner and a show**, creating a truly immersive experience.

Best Live Music Bars in Almería

- **Clasijazz** – A haven for **jazz lovers**, hosting **live performances** ranging from traditional jazz to **funk, soul, and world music**.
- **Madchester Club** – A must-visit for **rock and indie music fans**, offering **live bands and themed music nights**.
- **El Varadero** – A **seaside music bar** where you can enjoy **live Latin, reggae, and flamenco fusion** music.

From **traditional flamenco to modern live music**, Almería's music venues provide a **memorable night filled with rhythm and passion**.

12.3 Open-Air Cinemas and Cultural Performances

Almería's warm Mediterranean climate makes it **the perfect place for outdoor cultural events**, including **open-air cinemas, live theater, and summer concerts**. Watching a film under the stars or attending an **open-air performance in a historic square** is a magical way to spend an evening.

Best Open-Air Cinemas in Almería

- **Cine de Verano** – Held in **various locations throughout the city** during the summer months, featuring **Spanish and international films** in an **open-air setting**.
- **La Alcazaba Open-Air Cinema** – Imagine watching a movie with **Almería's medieval fortress** as a backdrop! This special event happens during cultural festivals.
- **Beach Screenings at Playa de San Miguel** – On summer nights, the **beach transforms into an open-air cinema**, where you can watch movies while feeling the **ocean breeze**.

Cultural Performances in Almería

- **Festival de Teatro en la Calle** – A **street theater festival** featuring **dramatic performances, acrobatics, and storytelling** in Almería's old town.
- **Noches en la Alcazaba** – A **series of nighttime concerts, poetry readings, and performances** held at the iconic **Alcazaba fortress**.

- **Carnaval de Almería** – A lively celebration with **parades, costumes, and live music**, bringing the streets to life.

For those who love **art, culture, and cinema**, Almería's **open-air entertainment scene** offers **unforgettable experiences under the night sky**.

12.4 Late-Night Tapas Culture

In Almería, **the night doesn't have to end at the bars and clubs**—one of the **best ways to experience the city after dark is through its famous tapas culture**. Unlike other Spanish cities, **Almería is one of the few places where you still get a free tapa with every drink**.

Best Late-Night Tapas Bars in Almería

- **Casa Puga** – An **iconic spot** for **classic Almerían tapas**, including **grilled prawns and jamón ibérico**.
- **La Mala** – A stylish gastrobar serving **creative fusion tapas with an international twist**.
- **De Tal Palo** – Famous for its **vegetarian tapas options and locally sourced ingredients**.
- **El Quinto Toro** – A traditional bar offering **bullfighting-themed decor and delicious tapas**.

Why Tapas Culture is Special in Almería

- Tapas **extend your night out**—locals hop from bar to bar, trying different dishes and socializing.
- You can enjoy a full meal **just by ordering drinks**, since each one comes with a tapa.
- It's an **affordable way to taste a variety of Spanish flavors** without committing to a full plate.

Whether you're enjoying **seafood, cured meats, or vegetarian delicacies**, Almería's **late-night tapas scene** is a must-experience part of the city's nightlife.

Chapter 13: Family-Friendly Almería

Almería is not just a destination for history lovers, beachgoers, or adventure seekers—it's also an **excellent place for families**. Whether you're traveling with young children, teenagers, or a multi-generational group, there's something for everyone. The city's **warm climate, safe environment, and variety of kid-friendly attractions** make it an ideal destination for a stress-free family vacation.

In this chapter, we'll explore:

- **The top attractions for kids** that blend fun and learning.
- **The best family beaches and outdoor parks** where children can run, play, and enjoy nature.
- **Interactive museums and educational activities** that will keep curious young minds engaged.
- **The best family-friendly accommodations** to ensure a comfortable stay for everyone.

Whether your family enjoys **outdoor adventures, cultural experiences, or simply relaxing by the sea**, Almería has plenty to offer.

13.1 Top Attractions for Kids

When traveling with children, keeping them entertained is a priority. Luckily, Almería offers a **variety of fun-filled attractions** that cater to kids of all ages. From **theme parks to nature reserves and historic fortresses**, here are some of the **best places for children in Almería**.

Oasys Mini Hollywood: A Wild West Adventure

If your kids love **cowboys, horses, and action-packed shows**, Oasys Mini Hollywood is the place to be. This **Western-themed park** was originally built as a film set for Hollywood productions and has since been transformed into an **interactive family attraction**.

- **Daily stunt shows** featuring cowboys, duels, and shootouts.
- **A mini-zoo** with over 200 species of animals, including giraffes, elephants, and exotic birds.
- **A swimming pool area** to cool off after a day of adventure.

The Alcazaba of Almería: A Journey Through Time

The **Alcazaba fortress** may not sound like an obvious choice for children, but its **vast open spaces, hidden tunnels, and ancient walls** make it an exciting place to explore. Kids can:

- **Pretend to be knights and princesses** as they wander through the medieval fortress.
- **Enjoy panoramic views** of the city and sea from the top of the walls.
- **Participate in guided tours** designed for families with engaging storytelling.

Mario Park: A Water Wonderland

If you're visiting Almería in the summer, **Mario Park in Roquetas de Mar** is a must-visit. This water park features:

- **Thrilling water slides** for older kids and teenagers.
- **Shallow pools and splash areas** for younger children.
- **Relaxing sunbeds and picnic areas** for parents to unwind.

Castillo de San Felipe: A Coastal Fortress

Located near the **Cabo de Gata Natural Park**, this **historical castle by the sea** is a great place for children to explore. The ruins spark **imagination and adventure**, and the location offers **stunning sea views**.

From action-packed parks to historic landmarks, **Almería provides endless excitement for young explorers**.

13.2 Family Beaches and Outdoor Parks

Almería is famous for its **beautiful coastline and natural landscapes**, making it a perfect place for families to **enjoy the outdoors**. The region's **gentle waves, soft sand, and well-equipped parks** ensure that both parents and children have a fantastic time.

Best Family-Friendly Beaches in Almería

- **Playa de San Miguel** – This **urban beach** is located close to Almería's city center and has **playgrounds, shallow waters, and plenty of beachfront cafes**.
- **Playa de las Salinas (Roquetas de Mar)** – A great beach for **building sandcastles, spotting flamingos, and enjoying calm waters**.
- **Playa de los Genoveses** – Located in **Cabo de Gata Natural Park**, this beach is ideal for families looking for a **peaceful, unspoiled beach** with crystal-clear waters.

Best Outdoor Parks for Families

- **Nicolás Salmerón Park** – This **tree-lined park** in the heart of the city is great for a **leisurely stroll, a picnic, or some playground fun**.
- **Parque de las Familias** – Specifically designed for children, this **huge park has themed play**

areas, slides, and water fountains** for hot days.
- **Cabo de Gata Natural Park** – For families who love **hiking, wildlife spotting, and nature walks**, this **protected area** is a must-visit.

Whether you prefer **relaxing at the beach or exploring nature**, Almería has outdoor spaces that are **perfect for family bonding**.

13.3 Interactive Museums and Educational Activities

For families looking to **blend fun with learning**, Almería offers a range of **interactive museums and cultural experiences** that engage young minds.

Best Museums for Kids in Almería

- **Almería Museum** – Features **archaeological exhibits**, including Roman and Moorish artifacts, making history exciting for children.
- **Casa del Cine** – A museum dedicated to **Almería's film history**, where kids can learn about the city's connection to Hollywood.
- **Museum of Olive Oil** – A fun way to introduce kids to **one of Spain's most important products** through hands-on activities and tastings.

Educational Activities for Families

- **Fossil Hunting in Sorbas Caves** – Explore **prehistoric caves filled with fossils** and learn about Almería's ancient past.
- **Astronomy at Calar Alto Observatory** – A perfect activity for kids who love space, with **telescopes and star-gazing experiences**.
- **Traditional Pottery Workshops** – Try your hand at making **Andalusian ceramics**, a fun way to engage kids in local culture.

These experiences ensure that children not only have fun but also leave Almería with **new knowledge and unforgettable memories**.

13.4 Best Family-Friendly Accommodations

Finding the right place to stay is essential for a **smooth and enjoyable family vacation**. Almería offers a variety of accommodations that cater to families, from **beachfront resorts to cozy apartments with kid-friendly amenities**.

Best Family Hotels in Almería

- **Barceló Cabo de Gata** – A beachfront hotel with **large family rooms, kids' pools, and entertainment programs**.

- **Playadulce Hotel** – Located in Aguadulce, this hotel features **water slides, a mini-club, and direct beach access**.
- **Ohtels Gran Hotel Almería** – A central hotel with **spacious suites and family-friendly services**.

Best Budget and Apartment-Style Accommodations

- **Apartamentos Torreluz** – Located in the **historic center**, offering **kitchen facilities for families who prefer self-catering**.
- **Camping Los Escullos** – A great option for families who love **nature and adventure**, with **bungalows, camping areas, and outdoor activities**.

With a variety of **hotels, apartments, and campgrounds**, Almería ensures that families find **comfortable and suitable accommodations**.

Chapter 14: Sustainable and Responsible Tourism in Almería

Almería, with its breathtaking landscapes, historic sites, and vibrant culture, is a **dream destination** for many travelers. However, with tourism comes responsibility—ensuring that our visits do not negatively impact the environment, local communities, or cultural heritage.

As travelers, we have the power to make a difference by embracing **sustainable and responsible tourism practices**. Whether it's through **eco-friendly travel choices, supporting local artisans, engaging in conservation efforts, or choosing ethical wildlife experiences**, we can contribute to preserving Almería's beauty for generations to come.

This chapter will explore:

- **Eco-friendly travel tips** to minimize our environmental footprint.
- **Ways to support local businesses and artisans**, helping communities thrive.
- **Ongoing conservation efforts in Almería** and how visitors can get involved.
- **Ethical wildlife and nature experiences** that respect the region's unique biodiversity.

Let's dive into how we can enjoy Almería responsibly while making a positive impact!

14.1 Eco-Friendly Travel Tips

Sustainable travel begins with small, conscious decisions that help reduce waste, conserve energy, and support eco-friendly initiatives. Here are some practical ways to travel more sustainably in Almería:

1. Choose Eco-Friendly Accommodations

- Look for **hotels and guesthouses with green certifications** (such as Biosphere, Green Key, or eco-labels).
- Stay in **locally owned boutique hotels or rural eco-lodges** that prioritize sustainability.
- Select accommodations that **use renewable energy sources, recycle waste, and reduce water consumption**.

2. Minimize Plastic Waste

- Bring a **reusable water bottle**—Almería has many places to refill it with clean drinking water.
- Carry a **cloth shopping bag** instead of using plastic bags at local markets.
- Say no to **single-use plastics** such as straws and cutlery—opt for reusable alternatives.

3. Reduce Your Carbon Footprint

- Use **public transport, bicycles, or walk** whenever possible instead of renting cars.
- If you need a car, **choose hybrid or electric vehicles** available at rental agencies.
- Take **direct flights** when possible, as take-offs and landings generate the most emissions.

4. Respect the Natural Environment

- Stay on **marked trails** while hiking to avoid damaging fragile ecosystems.
- Never leave trash behind—**"Leave No Trace"** should be every traveler's mantra.
- Avoid picking plants, disturbing wildlife, or touching corals in marine areas.

By making small changes in how we travel, we can **greatly reduce our impact on the environment** and help preserve Almería's natural beauty.

14.2 Supporting Local Businesses and Artisans

One of the best ways to be a responsible traveler is to **support the local economy**. Instead of spending money at large international chains, consider contributing directly to **small businesses, local artisans, and traditional markets**.

1. Shop at Local Markets

Almería is famous for its **bustling markets** that showcase local produce, handcrafted goods, and unique souvenirs. Some of the best places to shop include:

- **Mercado Central de Almería** – A great spot to buy fresh fruits, vegetables, and local cheeses.
- **Alcaicería Market** – A historical market offering handmade crafts, ceramics, and textiles.

By purchasing directly from artisans, travelers help preserve **traditional crafts and skills** while ensuring that money stays within the community.

2. Eat at Family-Owned Restaurants

Rather than dining at global fast-food chains, visitors should experience **authentic Almerían cuisine** at locally owned tapas bars and family-run eateries. Look for places that serve **traditional dishes made with local ingredients**.

Some highly recommended spots include:

- Casa Puga – A historic tapas bar serving
- **3. Stay in Locally Owned Accommodations**
- regional specialties since 1870.
- **La Gruta** – A cave restaurant offering a unique dining experience with locally sourced seafood and meats.

Instead of booking with large hotel chains, opt for **boutique hotels, family-run guesthouses, or rural**

eco-lodges. Not only does this help local entrepreneurs, but it also offers a **more personalized and unique experience**.

Supporting local businesses means **keeping money within the community**, fostering sustainable development, and preserving Almería's cultural identity.

14.3 Conservation Efforts in Almería

Almería is home to some of **Spain's most stunning natural landscapes**, but these environments require active conservation to protect them from over-tourism, pollution, and climate change. Several initiatives are working to preserve Almería's biodiversity and ecosystems.

1. Protecting Cabo de Gata-Níjar Natural Park

Cabo de Gata is one of Spain's most important protected areas. Conservation efforts focus on:

- **Preventing urban development** that threatens its fragile ecosystems.
- **Protecting marine life** by regulating fishing and preventing over-tourism in its waters.
- **Encouraging eco-friendly tourism**, such as hiking and sustainable diving.

2. Sea Turtle and Marine Life Conservation

Almería's coastline is home to **Loggerhead sea turtles**, dolphins, and other marine species. Organizations such as **Equinac** work to rescue injured sea creatures and promote awareness about **responsible marine tourism**.

How can visitors help?

- Avoid disturbing nesting areas.
- Choose **eco-friendly boat tours** that respect marine life.
- Reduce plastic waste to prevent ocean pollution.

3. Reforestation and Water Conservation

Due to its **semi-arid climate**, Almería faces challenges such as **desertification and water scarcity**. Several local projects focus on:

- **Replanting native trees and vegetation** to prevent soil erosion.
- **Using sustainable irrigation techniques** in agriculture.
- **Promoting responsible water use** among residents and tourists.

Travelers can support these efforts by visiting **eco-tourism centers**, joining volunteer programs, or simply **being mindful of their water consumption**.

14.4 Ethical Wildlife and Nature Experiences

Almería's natural landscapes provide **incredible opportunities to connect with wildlife**, but it's crucial to choose experiences that are **ethical and respectful** of nature.

1. Responsible Whale and Dolphin Watching

If you're planning a **boat tour**, choose companies that:

- Follow **strict guidelines** to avoid stressing marine life.
- Maintain a **safe distance** from animals.
- Never allow feeding or touching of wild creatures.

2. Birdwatching Without Disturbance

Almería is a birdwatcher's paradise, home to **flamingos, eagles, and migratory birds**. The best places for ethical birdwatching include:

- **Las Salinas de Cabo de Gata** – A saltwater lagoon that attracts thousands of flamingos.
- **Sierra de Alhamilla** – A mountain region home to rare birds of prey.

Travelers should **use binoculars instead of getting too close** and avoid loud noises that might disturb the wildlife.

3. Avoid Unethical Animal Tourism

While horseback riding in Almería's countryside can be ethical, avoid activities such as:

- **Zoos or attractions with caged wild animals.**
- **Performances involving exotic animals.**

Instead, choose **wildlife sanctuaries or conservation projects** that genuinely protect and rehabilitate animals.

Chapter 15: Practical Travel Information

Planning a trip to Almería goes beyond choosing where to stay and what to see. **Understanding transportation, safety measures, local customs, and**

budgeting tips can make your visit smoother and more enjoyable. This chapter covers essential **practical travel information** to help you navigate Almería with confidence.

You'll discover:

- **The best ways to get around Almería**, whether by bus, car, or bicycle.
- **Safety guidelines and emergency contacts** to ensure a worry-free trip.
- **Cultural norms and etiquette**, so you can interact respectfully with locals.
- **Smart budgeting tips** to make the most of your experience without overspending.

Let's dive into everything you need to know before traveling to Almería!

15.1 Transportation Options Within Almería

Almería offers a variety of **transportation options**, making it easy to explore the city and surrounding areas. Whether you prefer public transit, renting a car, or cycling, here's a breakdown of the best ways to get around.

1. Public Transportation: Affordable and Convenient

[Handwritten note: M-212 Almería — La Isleta del Moro, takes 1 hour]

Almería's public transport system is **efficient, budget-friendly, and eco-conscious**.

- **City Buses:** Operated by the company **Surbus**, Almería's buses connect major attractions, residential areas, and nearby beaches.
    - Tickets cost around **€1.05 per ride**, or you can buy a rechargeable **bus card** for savings on multiple trips.
    - Popular routes include those to **Cabo de Gata Natural Park and the University of Almería**.
    - Buses operate from **6:30 AM to 11:00 PM**, with some night buses on weekends.
- **Intercity Buses:** If you want to explore beyond Almería, **ALSA and Busbahnhof** offer frequent services to **Mojácar, Roquetas de Mar, and Granada**.

2. Taxis and Ride-Sharing: A Comfortable Option

- **Taxis are available throughout Almería**, with fares starting at around **€4** and increasing by distance.
- You can find taxis at **Plaza de las Flores, Almería Airport, and major hotels**.
- While Almería does not have **Uber**, local ride-sharing apps like **Cabify** operate in the city.

3. Renting a Car: The Best Choice for Road Trips

- Renting a car is ideal if you want to visit **hidden beaches, mountain villages, and the Tabernas Desert**.
- Car rentals start at **€30 per day**, and **an international driver's license is required** for non-EU travelers.
- Parking in Almería can be tricky—look for **"Zona Azul" (blue zones)**, which allow **paid parking for limited hours**.

4. Cycling and Walking: Eco-Friendly and Scenic

Almería's **flat terrain and coastal paths** make it a fantastic city to explore on foot or by bicycle.

- **Bike rentals cost around €10 per day**, with rental shops in **Plaza Vieja and Paseo Marítimo**.
- The **Paseo Marítimo bike lane** runs along the beach, offering beautiful views.
- Walking is a great way to explore the **Alcazaba, the Old Town, and Cathedral Square**.

15.2 Safety Tips and Emergency Contacts

Almería is generally a **safe city**, but it's always good to stay aware and prepared. Here are essential **safety tips and emergency numbers** to keep in mind.

1. General Safety Tips

- **Pickpocketing:** While rare, be mindful of your belongings in **crowded areas, markets, and public transport**.
- **Beach Safety:** Watch out for **strong currents**, especially at **unmonitored beaches**.
- **Sun Protection:** Almería's **hot summers** can be intense—always carry **sunscreen, water, and sunglasses**.
- **Emergency Situations:** If you feel unsafe, head to a **hotel, police station, or well-lit public area**.

2. Emergency Numbers

- **112** – General Emergency Number (Police, Fire, Ambulance)
- **091** – National Police
- **061** – Medical Emergency
- **085** – Fire Department
- **900 202 202** – Tourist Helpline (English-speaking assistance)

3. Healthcare and Pharmacies

- Almería has **high-quality hospitals and clinics**, with some offering **24-hour emergency services**.
- The best hospitals include **Hospital Universitario Torrecárdenas** and **Clínica Mediterráneo**.
- Pharmacies (**Farmacias**) are marked with a **green cross** and rotate **24-hour emergency services**.

15.3 Local Customs and Etiquette

Understanding **Almería's cultural norms** will help you interact respectfully with locals and immerse yourself in **Andalusian traditions**.

1. Greetings and Social Etiquette

- A common Spanish greeting is **a light kiss on both cheeks** (or a handshake for formal situations).
- People say **"Hola" (Hello) or "Buenos días" (Good morning)** when entering shops or restaurants.
- **"Gracias" (Thank you) and "Por favor" (Please)** are always appreciated.

2. Dining Customs

- **Lunch (La Comida)** is the main meal, typically eaten **between 2:00 PM and 4:00 PM**.
- **Dinner (La Cena)** is later than in many other countries, often starting **around 9:00 PM or 10:00 PM**.
- **Tipping isn't mandatory** in Spain, but leaving **5-10%** for excellent service is common.

3. Siesta Culture

- Many small businesses close for **siesta (2:00 PM – 5:00 PM)**, especially in summer.
- Larger shopping centers and restaurants **remain open** during siesta hours.

4. Dress Code and Religious Sites

- When visiting **churches and cathedrals**, wear **modest attire** (covering shoulders and knees).
- **Beachwear is for the beach**—walking around town in swimsuits is frowned upon.

Being aware of these cultural norms will **enhance your travel experience** and help you connect with locals

15.4 Budgeting and Cost-Saving Travel Tips

Almería is an affordable destination compared to other parts of Spain, but **smart planning** can stretch your budget further.

1. Affordable Accommodations

- **Hostels and Budget Hotels:** Prices start at **€20 per night** for dorm rooms.
- **Airbnb and Apartment Rentals:** Ideal for families or long stays, costing **€40-€80 per night**.
- **Off-Season Discounts:** Visit during **spring or autumn** for lower prices on hotels and flights.

2. Cheap Eats and Free Tapas

- Many tapas bars in Almería **offer free tapas** with a drink order—perfect for budget travelers!
- Visit **local markets** like Mercado Central for affordable fresh food and picnic supplies.
- Opt for **"Menú del Día" (Lunch Specials)** in restaurants, offering a full meal for **€10-€15**.

3. Free and Low-Cost Attractions

- The **Alcazaba of Almería** has free entry on Sundays.
- **Beaches, hiking trails, and coastal walks** are completely free.

- Many museums and cultural sites offer **discounted entry for students, seniors, and EU citizens**.

4. Transportation Savings

- Get a **bus pass** if using public transport frequently.
- Walking and cycling are **great budget-friendly alternatives**.
- Book intercity buses **in advance** for discounted fares.

With these tips, you can **enjoy Almería without overspending**, making your trip both affordable and unforgettable.

Chapter 16: Conclusion and Final Thoughts

As your journey through Almería comes to an end, it's time to reflect on the unforgettable experiences this Andalusian gem has offered. From its **sun-kissed beaches and historic fortresses to its vibrant festivals and exquisite cuisine**, Almería is a place that captures the heart of every traveler. Whether you came for the **rich cultural heritage, the breathtaking landscapes, or the warmth of its people**, there is no doubt that this city leaves an indelible mark.

In this final chapter, we'll look back at what makes Almería so special, provide resources for further reading, share **inspirational quotes** about the city, and encourage you to reflect on your own experiences.

16.1 Capturing the Spirit of Almería

Almería is more than just a destination—it's a feeling, an atmosphere, a story waiting to be told. It's the golden glow of the Alcazaba at sunset, the **swaying palm trees lining the Paseo de Almería**, and the echo of **flamenco music** drifting through a hidden courtyard.

The Essence of Almería in Three Words: Sun, Culture, and Authenticity

1. **Sun:**

- With over **300 days of sunshine a year**, Almería is a paradise for sunseekers. Whether you're lounging on the beaches of **Playa de los Genoveses** or hiking through the **rugged Tabernas Desert**, the sun is your constant companion.

2. **Culture:**

    - Almería's history is etched into its streets, from the towering **Alcazaba fortress** to the grand **Cathedral of Almería**. Moorish, Christian, and modern influences intertwine here, creating a rich cultural tapestry that invites exploration.

3. **Authenticity:**

    - Unlike some tourist-heavy destinations, Almería remains **true to itself**. Tapas bars still serve **free tapas with drinks**, local artisans continue **traditional crafts**, and life moves at a pace that invites visitors to slow down and savor every moment.

Unforgettable Experiences in Almería

- **Walking through the Old Town**, where whitewashed buildings and narrow alleys whisper stories of the past.

- **Exploring the natural beauty** of **Cabo de Gata-Níjar Natural Park**, where volcanic cliffs meet turquoise waters.
- **Immersing yourself in local festivals**, from the religious grandeur of **Semana Santa** to the lively street celebrations of the **Feria de Almería**.
- **Savoring the flavors of the region**, whether it's the famous **caldo quemado (burnt broth stew)** or a plate of **fresh seafood by the port**.

The spirit of Almería is one of discovery, warmth, and connection—something that stays with you long after you leave.

16.2 Resources for Further Reading

If your journey in Almería has sparked a deeper curiosity about its **history, culture, and traditions**, there are plenty of resources to continue exploring.

Books About Almería and Andalusia

- "South from Granada" – Gerald Brenan
    - A beautifully written account of life in a small Andalusian village in the 1920s, giving insight into the region's culture.
- "Almería: Tierra de Cine" – Various Authors

- ○ A fascinating look at Almería's role in the film industry, particularly its connection to Spaghetti Westerns.
- **"The Ornament of the World" – María Rosa Menocal**
  - ○ A deep dive into Spain's Islamic history, including insights into Almería's Moorish past.

Websites and Travel Guides

- **Spain's Official Tourism Website** (www.spain.info) – Up-to-date travel information on Almería and other Spanish destinations.
- **Andalucia.com** – A fantastic resource for exploring Andalusian culture, festivals, and travel tips.
- **Lonely Planet: Andalusia Guide** – Offers comprehensive travel advice and recommended itineraries for Almería and beyond.

Local Museums and Cultural Centers

- **Museo de Almería** – Showcasing prehistoric and Roman artifacts, providing deeper historical context.
- **Casa del Cine de Almería** – A must-visit for movie lovers interested in Almería's cinematic legacy.

- **Centro Andaluz de la Fotografía** – A unique cultural center highlighting Andalusian photography and visual storytelling.

Whether through books, websites, or local institutions, there's always more to learn about this remarkable city.

16.3 Inspirational Quotes About Almería

Sometimes, a single quote can capture the essence of a place better than a thousand words. Here are some **inspirational reflections** on Almería and Andalusia:

1. **"Almería is where the desert meets the sea, where time slows down, and where every sunset tells a different story."** – Anonymous Traveler
2. **"To walk through Almería is to walk through history, where Moorish walls whisper secrets, and the scent of orange blossoms lingers in the air."** – Local Poet
3. **"Spain's soul shines brightest in Andalusia, and Almería is its hidden jewel—a city of light, passion, and endless horizons."** – Travel Writer
4. **"Almería is not just a destination; it's a feeling, a memory, a longing to return."** – Anonymous

If you've visited Almería, you probably have your own words to describe it. What would your quote be?

16.4 Reflecting on Your Journey

Travel isn't just about the places you see—it's about how those places **change you**. As you reflect on your time in Almería, consider these questions:

1. What was the most memorable part of your trip?

- Was it standing on the **ramparts of the Alcazaba**, looking over the city?
- Or perhaps watching a **flamenco performance**, feeling the raw emotion of the dance?

2. What new things did you learn?

- Did you discover an appreciation for **Andalusian cuisine**?
- Did you gain insight into the **Moorish and Christian influences on Spain's history**?

3. How did Almería make you feel?

- Inspired?
- Relaxed?
- Connected to a culture and history that you hadn't experienced before?

Every journey leaves a mark, and **Almería has a way of lingering in the soul**. Whether it was the **taste of tapas, the warmth of the sun, or the echoes of history in the old streets**, this city becomes a part of those who visit.

Your Next Adventure

If Almería has sparked your love for **Andalusia**, why stop here? Consider exploring:

- **Granada** – Just a short trip away, home to the magnificent **Alhambra Palace**.
- **Seville** – The heart of flamenco and Andalusian tradition.
- **Córdoba** – A city of stunning **Moorish architecture**, including the breathtaking **Mezquita**.

Almería may be the end of this journey, but it's **just the beginning of many more**.

Final Thoughts

Almería is a city that **reveals its beauty slowly**, rewarding those who take the time to truly experience it. From its **ancient history to its modern-day charm**, it's a place that invites travelers to return again and again.

Whether you came for the **sun, the sea, the history, or the food**, you're now part of Almería's story. **May your**

memories of this magical city stay with you, and may your travels continue to inspire you.

Hasta luego, Almería—until we meet again.

Printed in Dunstable, United Kingdom